ALTERNATIVE INVESTMENTS WORKBOOK

CFA Institute is the premier association for investment professionals around the world, with over 170,000 members in more than 160 countries. Since 1963 the organization has developed and administered the renowned Chartered Financial Analyst® Program. With a rich history of leading the investment profession, CFA Institute has set the highest standards in ethics, education, and professional excellence within the global investment community, and is the foremost authority on investment profession conduct and practice. Each book in the CFA Institute Investment Series is geared toward industry practitioners along with graduate-level finance students and covers the most important topics in the industry. The authors of these cutting-edge books are themselves industry professionals and academics and bring their wealth of knowledge and expertise to this series.

ALTERNATIVE INVESTMENTS WORKBOOK

WILEY

ISBN 9781119853305 (Paperback)
ISBN 9781119853312 (ePDF)
ISBN 9781119853329 (ePub)

Printed in the United States of America

SKY10030646_101921

CONTENTS

CHAPTER 6
Hedge Fund Strategies   **51**

CHAPTER 7
Capital Market Expectations: Forecasting Asset Class Returns   **63**

CHAPTER 8
Asset Allocation to Alternative Investments   **75**

CHAPTER 9
Integrated Cases in Risk Management: Institutional   **87**

PART II
Solutions

CHAPTER 1
Introduction to Corporate Governance and Other ESG
Considerations   **91**

CHAPTER 2
Introduction to Alternative Investments   **93**

CHAPTER 3
Real Estate Investments   **101**

CHAPTER 4
Private Equity Investments   **109**

ALTERNATIVES WORKBOOK

LEARNING OBJECTIVES, SUMMARY OVERVIEW, AND PROBLEMS

INTRODUCTION TO CORPORATE GOVERNANCE AND OTHER ESG CONSIDERATIONS

LEARNING OUTCOMES

The candidate should be able to:

- describe corporate governance;
- describe a company's stakeholder groups, and compare interests of stakeholder groups;
- describe principal–agent and other relationships in corporate governance and the conflicts that may arise in these relationships;
- describe stakeholder management;
- describe mechanisms to manage stakeholder relationships and mitigate associated risks;
- describe functions and responsibilities of a company's board of directors and its committees;
- describe market and non-market factors that can affect stakeholder relationships and corporate governance;
- identify potential risks of poor corporate governance and stakeholder management, and identify benefits from effective corporate governance and stakeholder management;
- describe factors relevant to the analysis of corporate governance and stakeholder management;
- describe environmental and social considerations in investment analysis;
- describe how environmental, social, and governance factors may be used in investment analysis.

SUMMARY OVERVIEW

The investment community has increasingly recognized the importance of corporate governance as well as environmental and social considerations. Although practices concerning corporate governance (and ESG overall) will undoubtedly continue to evolve, investment analysts who have a good understanding of these concepts can better appreciate the implications of ESG considerations in investment decision making. The core concepts covered in this chapter are as follows:

- Corporate governance can be defined as a system of controls and procedures by which individual companies are managed.
- There are many systems of corporate governance, most reflecting the influences of either shareholder theory or stakeholder theory, or both. Current trends, however, point to increasing convergence.
- A corporation's governance system is influenced by several stakeholder groups, and the interests of the groups often diverge or conflict.
- The primary stakeholder groups of a corporation consist of shareholders, creditors, managers and employees, the board of directors, customers, suppliers, and government/regulators.
- A principal–agent relationship (or agency relationship) entails a principal hiring an agent to perform a particular task or service. In a corporate structure, such relationships often lead to conflicts among various stakeholders.
- Stakeholder management involves identifying, prioritizing, and understanding the interests of stakeholder groups and on that basis managing the company's relationships with stakeholders. The framework of corporate governance and stakeholder management reflects a legal, contractual, organizational, and governmental infrastructure.
- Mechanisms of stakeholder management may include general meetings, a board of directors, the audit function, company reporting and transparency, related-party transactions, remuneration policies (including say on pay), and other mechanisms to manage the company's relationship with its creditors, employees, customers, suppliers, and regulators.
- A board of directors is the central pillar of the governance structure, serves as the link between shareholders and managers, and acts as the shareholders' internal monitoring tool within the company.
- The structure and composition of a board of directors vary across countries and companies. The number of directors may vary, and the board typically includes a mix of expertise levels, backgrounds, and competencies.
- Executive (internal) directors are employed by the company and are typically members of senior management. Non-executive (external) directors have limited involvement in daily operations but serve an important oversight role.
- Two primary duties of a board of directors are duty of care and duty of loyalty.
- A company's board of directors typically has several committees that are responsible for specific functions and report to the board. Although the types of committees may vary across organization, the most common are the audit committee, governance committee, remuneration (compensation) committee, nomination committee, risk committee, and investment committee.
- Stakeholder relationships and corporate governance are continually shaped and influenced by a variety of market and non-market factors.

- Shareholder engagement by a company can provide benefits that include building support against short-term activist investors, countering negative recommendations from proxy advisory firms, and receiving greater support for management's position.
- Shareholder activism encompasses a range of strategies that may be used by shareholders when seeking to compel a company to act in a desired manner.
- From a corporation's perspective, risks of poor governance include weak control systems; ineffective decision making; and legal, regulatory, reputational, and default risk. Benefits include better operational efficiency, control, and operating and financial performance, as well as lower default risk (or cost of debt).
- Key analyst considerations in corporate governance and stakeholder management include economic ownership and voting control, board of directors representation, remuneration and company performance, investor composition, strength of shareholders' rights, and the management of long-term risks.
- ESG investment approaches range from *value*-based to *values*-based. There are six broad ESG investment approaches: Negative screening, Positive screening, ESG integration, Thematic investing, Engagement/active ownership, and Impact investing.
- Historically, environmental and social issues, such as climate change, air pollution, and societal impacts of a company's products and services, have been treated as negative externalities. However, increased stakeholder awareness and strengthening regulations are internalizing environmental and societal costs onto the company's income statement by responsible investors.

PROBLEMS

1. Corporate governance:
   A. complies with a set of global standards.
   B. is independent of both shareholder theory and stakeholder theory.
   C. seeks to minimize and manage conflicting interests between insiders and external shareholders.
2. Which group of company stakeholders would be *least* affected if the firm's financial position weakens?
   A. Suppliers
   B. Customers
   C. Managers and employees
3. Which of the following represents a principal–agent conflict between shareholders and management?
   A. Risk tolerance
   B. Multiple share classes
   C. Accounting and reporting practices
4. Which of the following issues discussed at a shareholders' general meeting would *most likely* require only a simple majority vote for approval?
   A. Voting on a merger
   B. Election of directors
   C. Amendments to bylaws

5. Which of the following statements regarding stakeholder management is *most* accurate?
   A. Company management ensures compliance with all applicable laws and regulations.
   B. Directors are excluded from voting on transactions in which they hold material interest.
   C. The use of variable incentive plans in executive remuneration is decreasing.

6. Which of the following represents a responsibility of a company's board of directors?
   A. Implementation of strategy
   B. Enterprise risk management
   C. Considering the interests of shareholders only

7. Which of the following statements about non-market factors in corporate governance is *most* accurate?
   A. Stakeholders can spread information quickly and shape public opinion.
   B. A civil law system offers better protection of shareholder interests than does a common law system.
   C. Vendors providing corporate governance services have limited influence on corporate governance practices.

8. Which of the following statements regarding corporate shareholders is *most* accurate?
   A. Cross-shareholdings help promote corporate mergers.
   B. Dual-class structures are used to align economic ownership with control.
   C. Affiliated shareholders can protect a company against hostile takeover bids.

9. Which of the following statements about environmental, social, and governance (ESG) in investment analysis is correct?
   A. ESG factors are strictly intangible in nature.
   B. ESG terminology is easily distinguishable among investors.
   C. Environmental and social factors have been adopted in investment analysis more slowly than governance factors.

10. Which of the following statements regarding ESG investment approaches is *most accurate*?
    A. Negative screening is the most commonly applied method.
    B. Thematic investing considers multiple factors.
    C. Positive screening excludes industries with unfavorable ESG aspects.

PART II

SOLUTIONS

INTRODUCTION TO CORPORATE GOVERNANCE AND OTHER ESG CONSIDERATIONS

SOLUTIONS

1. C is correct. Corporate governance is the arrangement of checks, balances, and incentives a company needs to minimize and manage the conflicting interests between insiders and external shareholders.
2. B is correct. Compared with other stakeholder groups, customers tend to be less concerned with, and affected by, a company's financial performance.
3. A is correct. Shareholder and manager interests can diverge with respect to risk tolerance. In some cases, shareholders with diversified investment portfolios can have a fairly high risk tolerance because specific company risk can be diversified away. Managers are typically more risk averse in their corporate decision making to better protect their employment status.
4. B is correct. The election of directors is considered an ordinary resolution and, therefore, requires only a simple majority of votes to be passed.
5. B is correct. Often, policies on related-party transactions require that such transactions or matters be voted on by the board (or shareholders), excluding the director holding the interest.
6. B is correct. The board typically ensures that the company has an appropriate enterprise risk management system in place.
7. A is correct. Social media has become a powerful tool for stakeholders to instantly broadcast information with little cost or effort and to compete with company management in influencing public sentiment.

8. C is correct. The presence of a sizable affiliated stockholder (such as an individual, family trust, endowment, or private equity fund) can shield a company from the effects of voting by outside shareholders.

9. C is correct. The risks of poor corporate governance have long been understood by analysts and shareholders. In contrast, the practice of considering environmental and social factors has been slower to take hold.

10. A is correct. Negative screening, which refers to the practice of excluding certain sectors, companies, or practices that violate accepted standards in such areas as human rights or environmental concerns, is the most common ESG investment approach.

INTRODUCTION TO ALTERNATIVE INVESTMENTS

LEARNING OUTCOMES

The candidate should be able to:

- describe types and categories of alternative investments;
- describe characteristics of direct investment, co-investment, and fund investment methods for alternative investments;
- describe investment and compensation structures commonly used in alternative investments;
- explain investment characteristics of hedge funds;
- explain investment characteristics of private capital;
- explain investment characteristics of natural resources;
- explain investment characteristics of real estate;
- explain investment characteristics of infrastructure;
- describe issues in performance appraisal of alternative investments;
- calculate and interpret returns of alternative investments on both before-fee and after-fee bases.

SUMMARY OVERVIEW

This chapter provides a comprehensive introduction to alternative investments. Some key points of the chapter are as follows:

- Alternative investments are supplemental strategies to traditional long-only positions in stocks, bonds, and cash. Alternative investments include investments in five main categories: hedge funds, private capital, natural resources, real estate, and infrastructure.

- Alternative investment strategies are typically active, return-seeking strategies that also often have risk characteristics different from those of traditional long-only investments.
- Characteristics common to many alternative investments, when compared with traditional investments, include the following: lower liquidity, less regulation, lower transparency, higher fees, and limited and potentially problematic historical risk and return data.
- Alternative investments often have complex legal and tax considerations and may be highly leveraged.
- Alternative investments are attractive to investors because of the potential for portfolio diversification resulting in a higher risk-adjusted return for the portfolio.
- Investors can access alternative invests in three ways:
  - Fund investment (such as a in a PE fund)
  - Direct investment into a company or project (such as infrastructure or real estate)
  - Co-investment into a portfolio company of a fund
- Investors conduct due diligence prior to investing in alternative investments. The due diligence approach depends on the investment method (direct, co-investing, or fund investing).
- Operational, financial, counterparty, and liquidity risks may be key considerations for those investing in alternative investments. These risks can be analyzed during the due diligence process. It is critical to perform fund due diligence to assess whether (a) the manager can effectively pursue the proposed investment strategy; (b) the appropriate organizational structure and policies for managing investments, operations, risk, and compliance are in place; and (c) the fund terms appear reasonable.
- Many alternative investments, such as hedge and private equity funds, use a partnership structure with a general partner that manages the business and limited partners (investors) who own fractional interests in the partnership.
- The general partner typically receives a management fee based on assets under management or committed capital (the former is common to hedge funds, and the latter is common to private equity funds) and an incentive fee based on realized profits.
- Hurdle rates, high-water marks, lockup and notice periods, and clawback provisions are often specified in the LPA.
- The fee structure affects the returns to investors (limited partners), with a waterfall representing the distribution method under which allocations are made to LPs and GPs. Waterfalls can be on a whole-of-fund basis (European) or deal-by-deal basis (American).
- Hedge funds are typically classified by strategy. One such classification includes four broad categories of strategies: equity hedge (e.g., market neutral), event driven (e.g., merger arbitrage), relative value (e.g., convertible bond arbitrage), macro and CTA strategies (e.g., commodity trading advisers).
- Funds-of-hedge-funds are funds that create a diversified portfolio of hedge funds. These vehicles are attractive to smaller investors that don't have the resources to select individual hedge funds and build a portfolio of them.
- Private capital is a broad term for funding provided to companies that is sourced from neither the public equity nor debt markets. Capital that is provided in the form of equity investments is called private equity, whereas capital that is provided as a loan or other form of debt is called private debt.
- Private equity refers to investment in privately owned companies or in public companies with the intent to take them private. Key private equity investment strategies include leveraged buyouts (e.g., MBOs and MBIs) and venture capital. Primary exit strategies include trade sale, IPO, and recapitalization.

- Private debt refers to various forms of debt provided by investors to private entities. Key private debt strategies include direct lending, mezzanine debt, and venture debt. Private debt also includes specialized strategies, such as CLOs, unitranche debt, real estate debt, and infrastructure debt.
- Natural resources include commodities (hard and soft), agricultural land (farmland), and timberland.
- Commodity investments may involve investing in actual physical commodities or in producers of commodities, but more typically, these investments are made using commodity derivatives (futures or swaps). One can also invest in commodities via a CTA (see hedge funds)
- Returns to commodity investing are based on changes in price and do not include an income stream, such as dividends, interest, or rent (apart from income earned on the collateral). However, timberland offers an income stream based on the sale of trees, wood, and other products. Timberland can be thought of as both a factory and a warehouse. Plus, timberland is a sustainable investment that mitigates climate-related risks.
- Farmland, like timberland, has an income component related to harvest quantities and agricultural commodity prices. However, farmland doesn't have the production flexibility of timberland, because farm products must be harvested when ripe.
- Real estate includes two major sectors: residential and commercial. Residential real estate is the largest sector, making up some 75% of the market globally. Commercial real estate primarily includes office buildings, shopping centers, and warehouses. Real estate property has some unique features compared with other asset classes, including heterogeneity (no two properties are identical) and fixed location.
- Real estate investments can be direct or indirect, in the public market (e.g., REITs) or private transactions, and in equity or debt.
- The assets underlying infrastructure investments are real, capital intensive, and long lived. These assets are intended for public use, and they provide essential services. Examples include airports, health care facilities, and power plants. Funding is often done on a public–private partnership basis.
- Social infrastructure assets are directed toward human activities and include such assets as educational, health care, social housing, and correctional facilities, with the focus on providing, operating, and maintaining the asset infrastructure.
- Infrastructure investments may also be categorized by the underlying asset's stage of development. Investing in infrastructure assets *that are to be constructed* is generally referred to as greenfield investment. Investing in *existing* infrastructure assets may be referred to as brownfield investment.
- Conducting performance appraisal on alternative investments can be challenging because these investments are often characterized by asymmetric risk–return profiles, limited portfolio transparency, illiquidity, product complexity, and complex fee structures.
- Traditional risk and return measures (such as mean return, standard deviation of returns, and beta) may provide an inadequate picture of alternative investments' risk and return characteristics. Moreover, these measures may be unreliable or not representative of specific investments.
- A variety of ratios can be calculated in order to review the performance of alternative investments, including the Sharpe ratio, Sortino ratio, Treynor ratio, Calmar ratio, and MAR ratio. In addition, batting average and slugging percentage can also be used. The IRR calculation is often used to evaluate private equity investments, and the cap rate is often used to evaluate real estate investments.

- Redemption rules and lockup periods can bring special challenges to performance appraisal of alternative investments.
- When comparing the performance of alternative investments versus an index, the analyst must be aware that indexes for alternative investments may be subject to a variety of biases, including survivorship and backfill biases.
- Analysts need to be aware of any custom fee arrangements in place that will affect the calculation of fees and performance. These can include such arrangements as fee discounts based on custom liquidity terms or significant asset size; special share classes, such as "founders' shares"; and a departure from the typical management fee + performance fee structure in favor of "either/or" fees.

PROBLEMS

1. Which of the following is *least likely* to be considered an alternative investment?
   A. Real estate
   B. Commodities
   C. Long-only equity funds
2. An investor is seeking an investment that can take long and short positions, may use multi-strategies, and historically exhibits low correlation with a traditional investment portfolio. The investor's goals will be *best* satisfied with an investment in:
   A. real estate.
   B. a hedge fund.
   C. a private equity fund.
3. Relative to traditional investments, alternative investments are *least likely* to be characterized by:
   A. high levels of transparency.
   B. limited historical return data.
   C. significant restrictions on redemptions.
4. Alternative investment funds are typically managed:
   A. actively.
   B. to generate positive beta return.
   C. assuming that markets are efficient.
5. Compared with traditional investments, alternative investments are *more likely* to have:
   A. greater use of leverage.
   B. long-only positions in liquid assets.
   C. more transparent and reliable risk and return data.
6. The potential benefits of allocating a portion of a portfolio to alternative investments include:
   A. ease of manager selection.
   B. improvement in the portfolio's risk–return relationship.
   C. accessible and reliable measures of risk and return.
7. From the perspective of the investor, the *most* active approach to investing in alternative investments is:
   A. co-investing.
   B. fund investing.
   C. direct investing.

8. In comparison to other alternative investment approaches, co-investing is *most likely*:
   A. more expensive.
   B. subject to adverse selection bias.
   C. the most flexible approach for the investor.

9. Relative to co-investing, direct investing due diligence is *most likely*:
   A. harder to control.
   B. more independent.
   C. equally thorough.

10. The investment method that typically requires the greatest amount of or most thorough due diligence from an investor is:
    A. fund investing.
    B. co-investing.
    C. direct investing.

11. An alternative investment fund's hurdle rate is a:
    A. rate unrelated to a catch-up clause.
    B. tool to protect clients from paying twice for the same performance.
    C. minimum rate of return the GP must exceed in order to earn a performance fee.

12. An investor in a private equity fund is concerned that the general partner can receive incentive fees in excess of the agreed-on incentive fees by making distributions over time based on profits earned rather than making distributions only at exit from investments of the fund. Which of the following is most likely to protect the investor from the general partner receiving excess fees?
    A. A high hurdle rate
    B. A clawback provision
    C. A lower capital commitment

13. Until the committed capital is fully drawn down and invested, the management fee for a private equity fund is based on:
    A. invested capital.
    B. committed capital.
    C. assets under management.

14. The distribution method by which profits generated by a fund are allocated between LPs and the GP is called:
    A. a waterfall.
    B. an 80/20 split.
    C. a fair division.

15. Fill in the blanks with the correct words: An American waterfall distributes performance fees on a(n) _____ basis and is more advantageous to the _____.
    A. deal-by-deal; LPs
    B. aggregate fund; LPs
    C. deal-by-deal; GP

16. Which approach is *most commonly* used by equity hedge strategies?
    A. Top down
    B. Bottom up
    C. Market timing

17. An investor may prefer a single hedge fund to a fund of funds if she seeks:
    A. due diligence expertise.
    B. better redemption terms.
    C. a less complex fee structure.

18. Hedge funds are similar to private equity funds in that both:
    A. are typically structured as partnerships.
    B. assess management fees based on assets under management.
    C. do not earn an incentive fee until the initial investment is repaid.
19. Both event-driven and macro hedge fund strategies use:
    A. long–short positions.
    B. a top-down approach.
    C. long-term market cycles.
20. Hedge fund losses are *most likely* to be magnified by a:
    A. margin call.
    B. lockup period.
    C. redemption notice period.
21. An equity hedge fund following a fundamental growth strategy uses fundamental analysis to identify companies that are *most likely* to:
    A. be undervalued.
    B. be either undervalued or overvalued.
    C. experience high growth and capital appreciation.
22. A collateralized loan obligation specialist is *most likely* to:
    A. sell its debt at a single interest rate.
    B. cater to niche borrowers in specific situations.
    C. rely on diverse risk profiles to complete deals.
23. Private capital is:
    A. accurately described by the generic term "private equity."
    B. a source of diversification benefits from both debt and equity.
    C. predisposed to invest in both the debt and equity of a client's firm.
24. The first stage of financing at which a venture capital fund *most likely* invests is the:
    A. seed stage.
    B. mezzanine stage.
    C. angel investing stage.
25. A private equity fund desiring to realize an immediate and complete cash exit from a portfolio company is *most likely* to pursue:
    A. an IPO.
    B. a trade sale.
    C. a recapitalization.
26. Angel investing capital is typically provided in which stage of financing?
    A. Later stage
    B. Formative stage
    C. Mezzanine stage
27. Private equity funds are *most likely* to use:
    A. merger arbitrage strategies.
    B. leveraged buyouts.
    C. market-neutral strategies.
28. A significant challenge to investing in timber is *most likely* its:
    A. high correlation with other asset classes.
    B. dependence on an international competitive context.
    C. return volatility compounded by financial market exposure.

29. A characteristic of farmland strongly distinguishing it from timberland is its:
    A. commodity price-driven returns.
    B. inherent rigidity of production for output.
    C. value as an offset to other human activities.
30. Which of the following statements about commodity investing is invalid?
    A. Few commodity investors trade actual physical commodities.
    B. Commodity producers and consumers both hedge and speculate.
    C. Commodity indexes are based on the price of physical commodities.
31. An investor seeks a current income stream as a component of total return and desires an investment that historically has low correlation with other asset classes. The investment *most likely* to achieve the investor's goals is:
    A. timberland.
    B. collectibles.
    C. commodities.
32. If a commodity's forward curve is downward sloping and there is little or no convenience yield, the market is said to be in:
    A. backwardation.
    B. contango.
    C. equilibrium.
33. The majority of real estate property may be classified as either:
    A. debt or equity.
    B. commercial or residential.
    C. direct ownership or indirect ownership.
34. Which of the following relates to a benefit when owning real estate directly?
    A. Taxes
    B. Capital requirements
    C. Portfolio concentration
35. Which of the following statements is true regarding mortgage-backed securities?
    A. Insurance companies prefer the first-loss tranche.
    B. When interest rates rise, prepayments will likely accelerate.
    C. When interest rates fall, the low-risk senior tranche will amortize more quickly.
36. Which of the following statements is true for REITs?
    A. According to GAAP, equity REITs are exempt from reporting earnings per share.
    B. Though equity REIT correlations with other asset classes are typically moderate, they are highest during steep market downturns.
    C. The REIT corporation pays taxes on income, and the REIT shareholder pays taxes on the REIT's dividend distribution of after-tax earnings.
37. What is the most significant drawback of a repeat sales index to measure returns to real estate?
    A. Sample selection bias
    B. Understatement of volatility
    C. Reliance on subjective appraisals
38. As the loan-to-value ratio increases for a real estate investment, risk *most likely* increases for:
    A. debt investors only.
    B. equity investors only.
    C. both debt and equity investors.

39. Compared with direct investment in infrastructure, publicly traded infrastructure securities are characterized by:
    A. higher concentration risk.
    B. more transparent governance.
    C. greater control over the infrastructure assets.
40. Which of the following forms of infrastructure investment is the most liquid?
    A. An unlisted infrastructure mutual fund
    B. A direct investment in a greenfield project
    C. An exchange-traded MLP
41. An investor chooses to invest in a brownfield, rather than a greenfield, infrastructure project. The investor is *most likely* motivated by:
    A. growth opportunities.
    B. predictable cash flows.
    C. higher expected returns.
42. The privatization of an existing hospital is best described as:
    A. a greenfield investment.
    B. a brownfield investment.
    C. an economic infrastructure investment.
43. Risks in infrastructure investing are *most likely* greatest when the project involves:
    A. construction of infrastructure assets.
    B. investment in existing infrastructure assets.
    C. investing in assets that will be leased back to a government.
44. The Sharpe ratio is a less-than-ideal performance measure for alternative investments because:
    A. it uses a semi-deviation measure of volatility.
    B. returns of alternative assets are not normally distributed.
    C. alternative assets exhibit low correlation with traditional asset classes.
45. Which of the following is true regarding private equity performance calculations?
    A. The money multiple calculation relies on the amount and timing of cash flows.
    B. The IRR calculation involves the assumption of two rates.
    C. Because private equity funds have low volatility, accounting conventions allow them to use a lagged mark-to-market process.
46. Which is *not* true of mark-to-model valuations?
    A. Return volatility may be understated.
    B. Returns may be smooth and overstated.
    C. A calibrated model will produce a reliable liquidation value.
47. An analyst wanting to assess the downside risk of an alternative investment is *least likely* to use the investment's:
    A. Sortino ratio.
    B. value at risk (VaR).
    C. standard deviation of returns.

48. United Capital is a hedge fund with $250 million of initial capital. United charges a 2% management fee based on assets under management at year end and a 20% incentive fee based on returns in excess of an 8% hurdle rate. In its first year, United appreciates 16%. Assume management fees are calculated using end-of-period valuation. The investor's net return assuming the performance fee is calculated net of the management fee is *closest* to:
    A. 11.58%.
    B. 12.54%.
    C. 12.80%.

49. Capricorn Fund of Funds invests GBP100 million in each of Alpha Hedge Fund and ABC Hedge Fund. Capricorn Fund of Funds has a "1 and 10" fee structure. Management fees and incentive fees are calculated independently at the end of each year. After one year, net of their respective management and incentive fees, Capricorn's investment in Alpha is valued at GBP80 million and Capricorn's investment in ABC is valued at GBP140 million. The annual return to an investor in Capricorn Fund of Funds, net of fees assessed at the fund-of-funds level, is *closest* to:
    A. 7.9%.
    B. 8.0%.
    C. 8.1%.

50. The following information applies to Rotunda Advisers, a hedge fund:
    • $288 million in AUM as of prior year end
    • 2% management fee (based on year-end AUM)
    • 20% incentive fee calculated:
        • net of management fee
        • using a 5% soft hurdle rate
        • using a high-water mark (high-water mark is $357 million)

    Current-year fund gross return is 25%.
    The total fee earned by Rotunda in the current year is *closest* to:
    A. $7.20 million.
    B. $20.16 million.
    C. $21.60 million.

51. A hedge fund has the following fee structure:

Annual management fee based on year-end AUM	2%
Incentive fee	20%
Hurdle rate before incentive fee collection starts	4%
Current high-water mark	$610 million

The fund has a value of $583.1 million at the beginning of the year. After one year, it has a value of $642 million before fees. The net percentage return to an investor for this year is *closest* to:
    A. 6.72%.
    B. 6.80%.
    C. 7.64%.

INTRODUCTION TO ALTERNATIVE INVESTMENTS

SOLUTIONS

1. C is correct. Long-only equity funds are typically considered traditional investments, and real estate and commodities are typically classified as alternative investments.
2. B is correct. Hedge funds may use a variety of strategies, generally have a low correlation with traditional investments, and may take long and short positions.
3. A is correct. Alternative investments are characterized as typically having low levels of transparency.
4. A is correct. There are many approaches to managing alternative investment funds, but typically these funds are actively managed.
5. A is correct. Investing in alternative investments is often pursued through such special vehicles as hedge funds and private equity funds, which have flexibility to use leverage. Alternative investments include investments in such assets as real estate, which is an illiquid asset, and investments in such special vehicles as private equity and hedge funds, which may make investments in illiquid assets and take short positions. Obtaining information on strategies used and identifying reliable measures of risk and return are challenges of investing in alternatives.
6. B is correct. Adding alternative investments to a portfolio may provide diversification benefits because of these investments' less-than-perfect correlation with other assets in the portfolio. As a result, allocating a portion of one's funds to alternatives could potentially result in an improved risk–return relationship. Challenges to allocating a portion of a portfolio to alternative investments include obtaining reliable measures of risk and return and selecting portfolio managers for the alternative investments.

7. C is correct. From the perspective of the investor, direct investing is the most active approach to investing because of the absence of fund managers and the services and expertise they generally provide.

A is incorrect because co-investing includes fund investing, which requires less due diligence compared with direct investing.

B is incorrect because fund investing in alternative assets demands less participation from the investor compared with the direct and co-investing approaches because an investor depends on the fund manager to identify, select, and manage the fund's investments.

8. B is correct. Co-investing may be subject to adverse selection bias. For example, the fund manager may make less attractive investment opportunities available to the co-investor while allocating its own capital to more appealing deals.

A is incorrect because co-investing is likely not more expensive than fund investing since co-investors can co-invest an additional amount alongside the fund directly in a fund investment without paying management fees on the capital that has been directly invested.

C is incorrect because direct investing, not co-investing, provides the greatest amount of flexibility for the investor.

9. B is correct. Direct investing due diligence may be more independent than that of co-investing because the direct investing team is typically introduced to opportunities by third parties rather than fund managers, as is customary in co-investing.

A is incorrect because the direct investing team has more control over the due diligence process compared with co-investing.

C is incorrect because due diligence for direct investing requires the investor to conduct a thorough investigation into the important aspects of a target asset or business, whereas in co-investing, fund managers typically provide investors with access to a data room so they can view the due diligence completed by the fund managers.

10. C is correct. Due diligence in direct investing will usually be more thorough and more rigid from an investor's perspective because of the absence of a fund manager that would otherwise conduct a large portion of the necessary due diligence.

11. C is correct. An alternative investment fund's hurdle rate is a minimum rate of return the GP must exceed in order to earn a performance fee.

A is incorrect because if a catch-up clause is included in the partnership agreement, the catch-up clause permits distributions in relation to the hurdle rate.

B is incorrect because it is a high-water mark (not a hurdle rate) that protects clients from paying twice for the same performance.

12. B is correct. A clawback provision requires the general partner in a private equity fund to return any funds distributed (to the general partner) as incentive fees until the limited partners have received their initial investments *and* the contracted portion of the total profits. A high hurdle rate will result in distributions occurring only after the fund achieves a specified return. A high hurdle rate decreases the likelihood of, but does not prevent, excess distributions. Management fees, not incentive fees, are based on committed capital.

13. B is correct. Until the committed capital is fully drawn down and invested, the management fee for a private equity fund is based on committed capital, not invested capital.

14. A is correct. Although profits are typically split 80/20 between LPs and the GP, the distribution method of profits is not called an "80/20 split." "Fair division" is not a real term that exists in the industry.

15. C is correct. American waterfalls, also known as deal-by-deal waterfalls, pay performance fees after every deal is completed and are more advantageous to the GP because they get paid sooner (compared with European, or whole-of-fund, waterfalls).

16. B is correct. Most equity hedge strategies use a bottom-up strategy.

    A is incorrect because most equity hedge strategies use a bottom-up (not top-down) strategy

    C is incorrect because most equity hedge strategies use a bottom-up (not market-timing) strategy.

17. C is correct. Hedge funds of funds have multi-layered fee structures, whereas the fee structure for a single hedge fund is less complex. Funds of funds presumably have some expertise in conducting due diligence on hedge funds and may be able to negotiate more favorable redemption terms than an individual investor in a single hedge fund could.

18. A is correct. Private equity funds and hedge funds are typically structured as partnerships where investors are limited partners and the fund is the general partner. The management fee for private equity funds is based on committed capital, whereas for hedge funds, the management fees are based on assets under management. For most private equity funds, the general partner does not earn an incentive fee until the limited partners have received their initial investment back.

19. A is correct. Long–short positions are used by both types of hedge funds to potentially profit from anticipated market or security moves. Event-driven strategies use a bottom-up approach and seek to profit from a catalyst event typically involving a corporate action, such as an acquisition or a restructuring. Macro strategies seek to profit from expected movements in evolving economic variables.

20. A is correct. Margin calls can magnify losses. To meet the margin call, the hedge fund manager may be forced to liquidate a losing position in a security, which, depending on the position size, could exert further price pressure on the security, resulting in further losses. Restrictions on redemptions, such as lockup and notice periods, may allow the manager to close positions in a more orderly manner and minimize forced-sale liquidations of losing positions.

21. C is correct. Fundamental growth strategies take long positions in companies identified, using fundamental analysis, to have high growth and capital appreciation. Fundamental value strategies use fundamental analysis to identify undervalued companies. Market-neutral strategies use quantitative and fundamental analysis to identify under- and over-valued companies.

22. C is correct. A CLO manager will extend several loans to corporations (usually to firms involved in LBOs, corporate acquisitions, or other similar types of transactions), pool these loans, and then divide that pool into various tranches of debt and equity that range in seniority and security. The CLO manager will then sell each tranche to different investors according to their risk profiles; the most senior portion of the CLO will be the least risky, and the most junior portion of the CLO (i.e., equity) will be the riskiest.

    A is incorrect because with the different CLO tranches having distinct risks varying with their seniority and security, they will be priced over a range of interest rates. In contrast, unitranche debt combines different tranches of secured and unsecured debt into a single loan with a single, blended interest rate.

    B is incorrect because debt extended to niche borrowers in specific situations is more commonly offered through specialty loans. For example, in litigation finance, a specialist funding company provides debt to a client to finance the borrower's legal fees and expenses in exchange for a portion of any case winnings.

23. B is correct. Investments in private capital funds can add diversity to a portfolio composed of publicly traded stocks and bonds because they have less-than-perfect correlation with those investments. There is also the potential to offer further diversification within the private capital asset class. For example, private equity investments may also offer vintage diversification since capital is not deployed at a single point in time but is invested over several years. Private debt provides investors with the opportunity to diversify the fixed-income portion of their portfolios since private debt investments offer more options than bonds and other public forms of traditional fixed income.

  A is incorrect because although private equity is considered by many to be the largest component of private capital, using "private equity" as a generic term could be less accurate and possibly misleading since other private forms of alternative finance have grown considerably in size and popularity.

  C is incorrect because although many private investment firms often have private equity and private debt arms, these teams typically won't invest in the same assets or businesses to avoid overexposure to a single investment.

24. A is correct. The seed stage supports market research and product development and is generally the first stage at which venture capital funds invest. The seed stage follows the angel investing stage. In the angel investing stage, funds are typically provided by individuals (often friends or family), rather than a venture capital fund, to assess an idea's potential and to transform the idea into a plan. Mezzanine-stage financing is provided by venture capital funds to prepare the portfolio company for its IPO.

25. B is correct. Private equity funds can realize an immediate cash exit in a trade sale. Using this strategy, the portfolio company is typically sold to a strategic buyer.

26. B is correct. Formative-stage financing occurs when the company is still in the process of being formed and encompasses several financing steps. Angel investing capital is typically raised in this early stage of financing.

27. B is correct. The majority of private equity activity involves leveraged buyouts. Merger arbitrage and market neutral are strategies used by hedge funds.

28. B is correct. A primary risk of timber is the international competitive landscape. Timber is a globally sold and consumed commodity subject to world trade interruptions. So the international context can be considered one of its major risk factors.

  A is incorrect because timberland offers an income stream based on the sale of trees, wood, and other timber products that has not been highly correlated with other asset classes.

  C is incorrect because investors are interested in timber because of its global nature (everyone requires shelter), the current income generated from the sale of the crop, inflation protection from holding the land, and its safe haven characteristics (it offers some insulation from financial market volatility).

29. B is correct. Unlike timberland products, farm products must be harvested when ripe, so there is little flexibility in the production process. In contrast, timber (trees) can be grown and easily "stored" by simply not harvesting. This feature offers the flexibility of harvesting more trees when timber prices are up and delaying harvests when prices are down.

  A is incorrect because just as a primary return driver for timberland is change in commodity price (of lumber from cut wood) in either the spot or futures price, farmland's returns are driven by agricultural commodity prices, with commodity futures contracts potentially combined with farmland holdings to generate an overall hedged return.

  C is incorrect because for both farmland and timberland owned or leased for the benefit of the bounty each generates in the form of crops and more broadly timber, since these resources consume carbon as part of the plant life cycle, the considered value comes not just from the harvest but also from the offset to other human activities.

30. C is correct. Commodity indexes typically use the price of futures contracts on the commodities included in them rather than the prices of the physical commodities themselves in order to be transparent, investable, and replicable.

    A is incorrect because trading in physical commodities is primarily limited to a smaller group of entities that are part of the physical supply chain. Thus, most commodity investors do not trade actual physical commodities but, rather, trade commodity derivatives.

    B is incorrect because although supply chain participants use futures to hedge their forward purchases and sales of the physical commodities, those commodity producers and consumers nonetheless both hedge and speculate on commodity prices.

31. A is correct. Timberland offers an income stream based on the sale of timber products as a component of total return and has historically generated returns not highly correlated with other asset classes.

32. B is correct. Contango is a condition in the futures markets in which the spot price is lower than the futures price, the forward curve is upward sloping, and there is little or no convenience yield. Backwardation is the opposite condition in the futures markets, where the spot price exceeds the futures price, the forward curve is downward sloping, and the convenience yield is high. Equilibrium is an economic term where supply is equal to demand.

33. B is correct. The majority of real estate property may be classified as either commercial or residential.

34. A is correct. When owning real estate directly, there is a benefit related to taxes. The owner can use property non-cash depreciation expenses to reduce taxable income and lower the current income tax bill. In fact, accelerated depreciation and interest expense can reduce taxable income below zero in the early years of asset ownership, and losses can be carried forward to offset future income. Thus, a property investment can be cash-flow positive while generating accounting losses and deferring tax payments. If the tax losses do not reverse during the life of the asset, depreciation-recapture taxes can be triggered when the property is sold.

    B is incorrect because the large capital requirement is a major disadvantage of investing directly in real estate.

    C is incorrect because a disadvantage for smaller investors who own real estate directly is that they bear the risk of portfolio concentration.

35. C is correct. When interest rates decline, borrowers are likely to refinance their loans at a faster pace than before, resulting in faster amortization of each MBS tranche, including the senior tranche, which is the lowest-risk tranche.

    A is incorrect because risk-averse investors, primarily insurance companies, prefer the lowest-risk tranches, which are the first to receive interest and principal. The junior-most tranche is referred to as the first-loss tranche. It is the highest-risk tranche and is the last to receive interest and principal distributions.

    B is incorrect because when interest rates rise, prepayments will likely slow down, lengthening the duration of most MBS tranches. Prepayments will likely increase when interest rates decline, because borrowers are likely to refinance their loans at a faster pace.

36. B is correct. Real estate investments, including REITs, provide important portfolio benefits due to moderate correlation with other asset classes. However, there are periods when equity REIT correlations with other securities are high, and their correlations are highest during steep market downturns.

A is incorrect because equity REITs, like other public companies, must report earnings per share based on net income as defined by GAAP or IFRS.

C is incorrect because REITs can avoid this double taxation. A REIT can avoid corporate income taxation by distributing dividends equal to 90%–100% of its taxable net rental income. This ability to avoid double taxation is the main appeal of the REIT structure.

37. A is correct. A repeat sales index uses the changes in price of repeat sales properties to construct the index. Sample selection bias is a significant drawback because the properties that sell in each period vary and may not be representative of the overall market the index is meant to cover. The properties that transact are not a random sample and may be biased toward properties that changed in value. Understated volatility and reliance on subjective appraisals by experts are drawbacks of an appraisal index.

38. C is correct. The higher the loan-to-value ratio, the higher leverage is for a real estate investment, which increases the risk to both debt and equity investors.

39. B is correct. Publicly traded infrastructure securities, which include shares of companies, exchange-traded funds, and listed funds that invest in infrastructure, provide the benefits of transparent governance, liquidity, reasonable fees, market prices, and the ability to diversify among underlying assets. Direct investment in infrastructure involves a large capital investment in any single project, resulting in high concentration risks. Direct investment in infrastructure provides control over the assets and the opportunity to capture the assets' full value.

40. C is correct. A publicly traded infrastructure security, such as an exchange-traded MLP, provides the benefit of liquidity.

41. B is correct. A brownfield investment is an investment in an existing infrastructure asset, which is more likely to have a history of steady cash flows compared with that of a greenfield investment. Growth opportunities and returns are expected to be lower for brownfield investments, which are less risky than greenfield investments.

42. B is correct. Investing in an existing infrastructure asset with the intent to privatize, lease, or sell and lease back the asset is referred to as a brownfield investment. An economic infrastructure asset supports economic activity and includes such assets as transportation and utility assets. Hospitals are social infrastructure assets, which are focused on human activities.

43. A is correct. Infrastructure projects involving construction have more risk than investments in existing assets with a demonstrated cash flow or investments in assets that are expected to generate regular cash flows.

44. B is correct. The Sharpe ratio assumes normally distributed returns. However, alternative assets tend to have non-normal return distributions with significant skewness (fat tails in one direction or the other) and kurtosis (sharper peak than a normal distribution has, with fatter tails). Therefore, the Sharpe ratio may not be a good risk-adjusted performance measure to rely on for alternative investments.

A is incorrect because the Sharpe ratio does not use a semi-deviation measure of volatility; it uses standard deviation. The Sortino ratio uses a semi-deviation measure of volatility. Further, the use of semi-deviation instead of standard deviation actually makes the Sortino ratio a more attractive measure of alternative asset performance than the Sharpe ratio.

C is incorrect because correlation does not enter into the calculation of the Sharpe ratio. However, it is true that alternative assets can have low correlations with other asset classes. In contrast to the Sharpe ratio, the Treynor ratio incorporates the beta of the alternative asset relative to a benchmark, which is conceptually similar to correlation.

45. B is correct. The determination of an IRR involves certain assumptions about a financing rate to use for outgoing cash flows (typically a weighted average cost of capital) and a reinvestment rate assumption to make on incoming cash flows (which must be assumed and may or may not actually be earned).

    A is incorrect because the money multiple calculation completely ignores the timing of cash flows.

    C is incorrect because it is somewhat of a reversal of cause and effect: Private equity (PE) funds can appear to have low volatility because of the lag in their mark-to-market process. It's not that PE investments don't actually rise and fall behind the scenes with economic influences, but accounting conventions may simply leave longer-lived investments marked at their initial cost for some time or with only modest adjustments to such carrying value until known impairments or realization events begin to transpire. Also, because PE funds are not easily marked to market, their returns can appear somewhat smoothed, making them appear more resilient and less correlated with other assets than they really are. The slowness to re-mark them can unfortunately be confused by investors as an overall lack of volatility.

46. C is correct. It is not true that a calibrated model will produce a reliable liquidation value in a mark-to-model valuation. The need to use a model for valuation arises when an asset is so illiquid that there are not reliable market values available. A model may reflect only an imperfect theoretical valuation, not a true liquidation value, should liquidation become necessary. The illiquid nature of alternative assets means that estimates, rather than observable transaction prices, may have been used for valuation purposes.

    A and B are not correct because they are both true statements.

47. C is correct. Downside risk measures focus on the left side of the return distribution curve, where losses occur. The standard deviation of returns assumes that returns are normally distributed. Many alternative investments do not exhibit close-to-normal distributions of returns, which is a crucial assumption for the validity of a standard deviation as a comprehensive risk measure. Assuming normal probability distributions when calculating these measures will lead to an underestimation of downside risk for a negatively skewed distribution. Both the Sortino ratio and the VaR measure are measures of downside risk.

48. B is correct. The net investor return is 12.54%, calculated as follows:

    End-of-year capital = $250 million × 1.16 = $290 million.
    Management fee = $290 million × 2% = $5.8 million.
    Hurdle amount = 8% of $250 million = $20 million.
    Incentive fee = ($290 − $250 − $20 − $5.8) million × 20% = $2.84 million.
    Total fees to United Capital = ($5.8 + $2.84) million = $8.64 million.
    Investor net return: ($290 − $250 − $8.64)/$250 = 12.54%.

49. A is correct because the net investor return is 7.9%, calculated as follows:

    First, note that "1 and 10" refers to a 1% management fee and a 10% incentive fee.
    End-of-year capital = GBP140 million + GBP80 million = GBP220 million.
    Management fee = GBP220 million × 1% = GBP2.2 million.
    Incentive fee = (GBP220 − GBP200) million × 10% = GBP2 million.
    Total fees to Capricorn = (GBP2.2 + GBP2) million = GBP4.2 million.
    Investor net return: (GBP220 − GBP200 − GBP4.2)/GBP200 = 7.9%.

50. A is correct. Although the gross return of Rotunda results in a $360 million gross NAV, the deduction of the $7.2 million incentive fee brings NAV to $352.8 million, which is below the prior high-water mark. Rotunda earns a management fee of $7.20 million but does not earn an incentive fee because the year-end fund value net of management fee does not exceed the prior high-water mark of $357 million. Since Rotunda is still also below the prior-year high-water mark, the hurdle rate of return is also basically irrelevant in this fee calculation.

The specifics of this calculation are as follows:

End-of-year AUM = Prior year-end AUM × (1 + Fund return) = $288 million × 1.25 = $360 million.
$360 million × 2% = $7.20 million management fee.
$360 million − $7.2 million = $352.8 million AUM net of management fee.

The year-end AUM net of fees do not exceed the $357 million high-water mark. Therefore, no incentive fee is earned.

51. C is correct. The management fee for the year is

$642 × 0.02 = $12.84 million.

Because the ending gross value of the fund of $642 million exceeds the high-water mark of $610 million, the hedge fund can collect an incentive fee on gains above this high-water mark but net of the hurdle rate of return. The incentive fee calculation becomes

{$642 − [$610 × (1 + 0.04)]} × 0.20 = $1.52 million.

The net return to the investor for the year is

[($642 − $12.84 − $1.52)/$583.1] − 1 ≈ 0.07638 ≈ 7.64%.

CHAPTER 3

REAL ESTATE INVESTMENTS

LEARNING OUTCOMES

The candidate should be able to:

- compare the characteristics, classifications, principal risks, and basic forms of public and private real estate investments;
- explain portfolio roles and economic value determinants of real estate investments;
- discuss commercial property types, including their distinctive investment characteristics;
- explain the due diligence process for both private and public equity real estate investments;
- discuss real estate investment indexes, including their construction and potential biases;
- discuss the income, cost, and sales comparison approaches to valuing real estate properties;
- compare the direct capitalization and discounted cash flow valuation methods;
- estimate and interpret the inputs (for example, net operating income, capitalization rate, and discount rate) to the direct capitalization and discounted cash flow valuation methods;
- calculate the value of a property using the direct capitalization and discounted cash flow valuation methods;
- calculate and interpret financial ratios used to analyze and evaluate private real estate investments;
- discuss types of REITs;
- justify the use of net asset value per share (NAVPS) in REIT valuation and estimate NAVPS based on forecasted cash net operating income;
- describe the use of funds from operations (FFO) and adjusted funds from operations (AFFO) in REIT valuation;
- calculate and interpret the value of a REIT share using the net asset value, relative value (price-to-FFO and price-to-AFFO), and discounted cash flow approaches; and
- explain advantages and disadvantages of investing in real estate through publicly traded securities compared to private vehicles.

SUMMARY OVERVIEW

Real estate property is an asset class that plays a significant role in many investment portfolios and is an attractive source of current income. Investor allocations to public and private real estate have increased significantly over the last 20 years. Because of the unique characteristics of real estate property, real estate investments tend to behave differently from other asset classes—such as stocks, bonds, and commodities—and thus have different risks and diversification benefits. Private real estate investments are further differentiated because the investments are not publicly traded and require analytic techniques different from those of publicly traded assets. Because of the lack of transactions, the appraisal process is required to value real estate property. Many of the indexes and benchmarks used for private real estate also rely on appraisals, and because of this characteristic, they behave differently from indexes for publicly traded equities, such as the S&P 500, MSCI Europe, FTSE Asia Pacific, and many other regional and global indexes.

General Characteristics of Real Estate

- Real estate investments make up a significant portion of the portfolios of many investors.
- Real estate investments can occur in four basic forms: private equity (direct ownership), publicly traded equity (indirect ownership claim), private debt (direct mortgage lending), and publicly traded debt (securitized mortgages).
- Each of the basic forms of real estate investment has its own risks, expected returns, regulations, legal structures, and market structures.
- Equity investors generally expect a higher rate of return than lenders (debt investors) because they take on more risk. The returns to equity real estate investors have two components: an income stream and capital appreciation.
- Many motivations exist for investing in real estate income property. The key ones are current income, price appreciation, inflation hedge, diversification, and tax benefits.
- Adding equity real estate investments to a traditional portfolio will potentially have diversification benefits because of the less-than-perfect correlation of equity real estate returns with returns to stocks and bonds.
- If the income stream can be adjusted for inflation and real estate prices increase with inflation, then equity real estate investments may provide an inflation hedge.
- Debt investors in real estate expect to receive their return from promised cash flows and typically do not participate in any appreciation in value of the underlying real estate. Thus, debt investments in real estate are similar to other fixed-income investments, such as bonds.
- Regardless of the form of real estate investment, the value of the underlying real estate property can affect the performance of the investment. Location is a critical factor in determining the value of a real estate property.
- Real estate property has some unique characteristics compared with other investment asset classes. These characteristics include heterogeneity and fixed location, high unit value, management intensiveness, high transaction costs, depreciation, sensitivity to the credit market, illiquidity, and difficulty of value and price determination.
- There are many different types of real estate properties in which to invest. The main commercial (income-producing) real estate property types are office, industrial and warehouse, retail, and multi-family. Other types of commercial properties are typically classified by their specific use.
- Certain risk factors are common to commercial property, but each property type is likely to have a different susceptibility to these factors. The key risk factors that can affect commercial

- real estate include business conditions, lead time for new development, excess supply, cost and availability of capital, unexpected inflation, demographics, lack of liquidity, environmental issues, availability of information, management expertise, and leverage.
- Location, lease structures, and economic factors—such as economic growth, population growth, employment growth, and consumer spending—affect the value of each property type.
- An understanding of the lease structure is important when analyzing a real estate investment.
- Appraisals estimate the value of real estate income property. Definitions of value include market value, investment value, value in use, and mortgage lending value.
- Due diligence investigates factors that might affect the value of a property prior to making or closing on an investment. These factors include leases and lease history, operating expenses, environmental issues, structural integrity, lien/proof of ownership, property tax history, and compliance with relevant laws and regulations.
- Appraisal-based and transaction-based indexes are used to track the performance of private real estate. Appraisal-based indexes tend to lag transaction-based indexes and appear to have lower volatility and lower correlation with other asset classes than transaction-based indexes.

Private Equity Real Estate

- Generally, three different approaches are used by appraisers to estimate value: income, cost, and sales comparison.
- The income approach includes direct capitalization and discounted cash flow methods. Both methods focus on net operating income as an input to the value of a property and indirectly or directly factor in expected growth.
- The cost approach estimates the value of a property based on adjusted replacement cost. This approach is typically used for unusual properties for which market comparables are difficult to obtain.
- The sales comparison approach estimates the value of a property based on what price comparable properties are selling for in the current market.
- When debt financing is used to purchase a property, additional ratios and returns calculated and interpreted by debt and equity investors include the loan-to-value ratio, the debt service coverage ratio, and leveraged and unleveraged internal rates of return.

Publicly Traded Real Estate Securities

- The principal types of publicly traded real estate securities available globally are real estate investment trusts, real estate operating companies, and residential and commercial mortgage-backed securities.
- Publicly traded equity real estate securities offer investors participation in the returns from investment real estate with the advantages of superior liquidity; greater potential for diversification by property, geography, and property type; access to a larger range of properties; the benefit of management services; limited liability; protection accorded by corporate governance, disclosure, and other securities regulations; and in the case of REITs, exemption from corporate income taxation within the REIT if prescribed requirements are met.
- Disadvantages include the costs of maintaining a publicly traded corporate structure and complying with regulatory filings, pricing determined by the stock market and returns that can be volatile, the potential for structural conflicts of interest, and tax differences compared with direct ownership of property that can be disadvantageous under some circumstances.

- Compared with other publicly traded shares, REITs offer higher-than-average yields and greater stability of income and returns. They are amenable to a net asset value approach to valuation because of the existence of active private markets for their real estate assets. Compared with REOCs, REITs offer higher yields and income tax exemptions but have less operating flexibility to invest in a broad range of real estate activities and less potential for growth from reinvesting their operating cash flows because of their high income-to-payout ratios.
- In assessing the investment merits of REITs, investors analyze the effects of trends in general economic activity, retail sales, job creation, population growth, and new supply and demand for specific types of space. They also pay particular attention to occupancies, leasing activity, rental rates, remaining lease terms, in-place rents compared with market rents, costs to maintain space and re-lease space, tenants' financial health and tenant concentration in the portfolio, financial leverage, debt maturities and costs, and the quality of management and governance.
- Analysts make adjustments to the historical cost-based financial statements of REITs and REOCs to obtain better measures of current income and net worth. The three principal figures they calculate and use are (1) funds from operations or accounting net earnings, excluding depreciation, deferred tax charges, and gains or losses on sales of property and debt restructuring; (2) adjusted funds from operations, or funds from operations adjusted to remove straight-line rent and to provide for maintenance-type capital expenditures and leasing costs, including leasing agents' commissions and tenants' improvement allowances; and (3) net asset value or the difference between a real estate company's asset and liability ranking prior to shareholders' equity, all valued at market values instead of accounting book values.
- REITs and some REOCs generally return a significant portion of their income to their investors and, as a result, tend to pay high dividends. Thus, dividend discount or discounted cash flow models for valuation are also applicable. These valuation approaches are applied in the same manner as they are for shares in other industries. Usually, investors use two- or three-step dividend discount models with near-term, intermediate-term, and/or long-term growth assumptions. In discounted cash flow models, investors often use intermediate-term cash flow projections and a terminal value based on historical cash flow multiples.

PROBLEMS

The following information relates to Questions 1–12.

Amanda Rodriguez is an alternative investment analyst for a US investment management firm, Delphinus Brothers. Delphinus's chief investment officer, Michael Tang, has informed Rodriguez that he wants to reduce the amount invested in traditional asset classes and gain exposure to the real estate sector by acquiring commercial property in the United States. Rodriguez is asked to analyze potential commercial real estate investments for Delphinus Brothers. Selected data on three commercial real estate properties are presented in Exhibit 1.

EXHIBIT 1   Selected Property Data

	Property 1	Property 2	Property 3
Property Type	Downtown Office Building	Grocery-Anchored Retail Center	Multi-Family Building
Location	New York City	Miami	Boston
Occupancy	90.00%	93.00%	95.00%
Square Feet or Number of Units	100,000 sf	205,000 sf	300 units
Gross Potential Rent	$4,750,000	$1,800,000	$3,100,000
Expense Reimbursement Revenue	$333,333	$426,248	$0
Other Income (includes % rent)	$560,000	$15,000	$45,000
Potential Gross Income	$5,643,333	$2,241,248	$3,145,000
Vacancy Loss	($564,333)	($156,887)	($157,250)
Effective Gross Income	$5,079,000	$2,084,361	$2,987,750
Property Management Fees	($203,160)	($83,374)	($119,510)
Other Operating Expenses	($2,100,000)	($342,874)	($1,175,000)
Net Operating Income	$2,775,840	$1,658,113	$1,693,240

Rodriguez reviews the three properties with Tang, who indicates that he would like her to focus on Property 1 because of his prediction of robust job growth in New York City over the next 10 years. To complete her analysis, Rodriquez assembles additional data on Property 1, which is presented in Exhibits 2, 3, and 4.

As part of the review, Tang asks Rodriguez to evaluate financing alternatives to determine whether it would be better to use debt financing or to make an all-cash purchase. Tang directs Rodriguez to inquire about terms with Richmond Life Insurance Company, a publicly traded company that is an active lender on commercial real estate property. Rodriguez obtains the following information from Richmond Life for a loan on Property 1: loan term of five years, interest rate of 5.75% interest only, maximum loan to value of 75%, and minimum debt service coverage ratio of 1.5×. Data on Property 1 are provided in Exhibit 2, Exhibit 3, and Exhibit 4.

EXHIBIT 2   Six-Year Net Operating Income (NOI) and DCF Assumptions for Property 1

	Year 1	Year 2	Year 3	Year 4	Year 5	Year 6
NOI	$2,775,840	$2,859,119	$2,944,889	$3,033,235	$3,124,232	$3,217,959

DCF Assumptions

Investment Hold Period	5 years
Going-In Cap Rate	5.25%
Terminal Cap Rate	6.00%
Discount Rate	7.25%
Income/Value Growth Rate	Constant

EXHIBIT 3   Sales Comparison Data for Property 1

Variable	Property 1	Sales Comp A	Sales Comp B	Sales Comp C
Age (years)	10	5	12	25
Condition	Good	Excellent	Good	Average
Location	Prime	Secondary	Secondary	Prime
Sale Price psf		$415 psf	$395 psf	$400 psf
Adjustments				
Age (years)		−10%	2%	10%
Condition		−10%	0%	10%
Location		15%	15%	0%
Total Adjustments		−5%	17%	20%

EXHIBIT 4   Other Selected Data for Property 1

Land Value	$7,000,000
Replacement Cost	$59,000,000
Total Depreciation	$5,000,000

After reviewing her research materials, Rodriguez formulates the following two conclusions:

Conclusion 1: Benefits of private equity real estate investments include the owners' ability to attain diversification benefits, to earn current income, and to achieve tax benefits.

Conclusion 2: Risk factors of private equity real estate investments include business conditions, demographics, the cost of debt and equity capital, and financial leverage.

1. Which of the following is *most likely* accurate regarding Property 2, described in Exhibit 1?
   A. Operating expense risk is borne by the owner.
   B. The lease term for the largest tenant is longer than three years.
   C. A significant amount of percentage rent is linked to sales levels.
2. Based on Exhibits 2, 3, and 4, which of the following statements is *most* accurate regarding the valuation of Property 1?
   A. The cost approach valuation is $71 million.
   B. The adjusted price psf for Sales Comp B is $423 psf.
   C. The terminal value at the end of Year 5 in the income approach is $53,632,650.
3. Based on Exhibit 2, the growth rate of Property 1 is *closest* to:
   A. 0.75%.
   B. 1.25%.
   C. 2.00%.
4. Based on Exhibit 2, the value of Property 1 using the discounted cash flow method is *closest* to:
   A. $48,650,100.
   B. $49,750,900.
   C. $55,150,300.

5. Based on Exhibit 2, relative to the estimated value of Property 1 under the discounted cash flow method, the estimated value of Property 1 using the direct capitalization method is:
   A. the same.
   B. lower.
   C. higher.

6. Based on Exhibits 1 and 3, the estimated value of Property 1 using the sales comparison approach (assigning equal weight to each comparable) is *closest* to:
   A. 40,050,000.
   B. 40,300,000.
   C. 44,500,000.

7. In the event that Delphinus purchases Property 2, the due diligence process would *most likely* require a review of:
   A. all tenant leases.
   B. tenant sales data.
   C. the grocery anchor lease.

8. Compared with an all-cash purchase, a mortgage on Property 1 through Richmond Life would *most likely* result in Delphinus earning:
   A. a lower return on equity.
   B. a higher return on equity.
   C. the same return on equity.

9. Assuming an appraised value of $48 million, Richmond Life Insurance Company's maximum loan amount on Property 1 would be *closest* to:
   A. $32 million.
   B. $36 million.
   C. $45 million.

10. Rodriguez's Conclusion 1 is:
    A. correct.
    B. incorrect, because tax benefits do not apply to tax-exempt entities.
    C. incorrect, because private real estate is highly correlated with stocks.

11. Rodriguez's Conclusion 2 is:
    A. correct.
    B. incorrect, because inflation is not a risk factor.
    C. incorrect, because the cost of equity capital is not a risk factor.

12. Richmond Life Insurance Company's potential investment would *most likely* be described as:
    A. private real estate debt.
    B. private real estate equity.
    C. publicly traded real estate debt.

The following information relates to Questions 13–28.

First Life Insurance Company, Ltd., a life insurance company located in the United Kingdom, maintains a stock and bond portfolio and also invests in all four quadrants of the real estate market: private equity, public equity, private debt, and public debt. Each of the four real estate quadrants has a manager assigned to it. First Life intends to increase its allocation to real estate. The chief investment officer (CIO) has scheduled a meeting with the four real estate managers to discuss the allocation to real estate and to each real estate quadrant. Leslie Green, who manages the private equity quadrant, believes her quadrant offers the greatest potential and has identified three investment properties to consider for acquisition. Selected information for the three properties is presented in Exhibit 5.

EXHIBIT 5   Selected Information on Potential Private Equity Real Estate Investments

	Property		
	A	B	C
Property description	Single-Tenant Office	Shopping Center	Warehouse
Size (square meters)	3,000	5,000	9,000
Lease type	Net	Gross	Net
Expected loan-to-value ratio	70%	75%	80%
Total economic life	50 years	30 years	50 years
Remaining economic life	30 years	23 years	20 years
Rental income (at full occupancy)	£575,000	£610,000	£590,000
Other income	£27,000	£183,000	£29,500
Vacancy and collection loss	£0	£61,000	£59,000
Property management fee	£21,500	£35,000	£22,000
Other operating expenses	£0	£234,000	£0
Discount rate	11.5%	9.25%	11.25%
Growth rate	2.0%	See Assumption 2	3.0%
Terminal cap rate		11.00%	
Market value of land	£1,500,000	£1,750,000	£4,000,000
Replacement costs			
• Building costs	£8,725,000	£4,500,000	£12,500,000
• Developer's profit	£410,000	£210,000	£585,000
Deterioration—curable and incurable	£4,104,000	£1,329,000	£8,021,000
Obsolescence			
• Functional	£250,000	£50,000	£750,000
• Locational	£500,000	£200,000	£1,000,000
• Economic	£500,000	£100,000	£1,000,000
Comparable adjusted price per square meter			
• Comparable Property 1	£1,750	£950	£730
• Comparable Property 2	£1,825	£1,090	£680
• Comparable Property 3	£1,675	£875	£725

To prepare for the upcoming meeting, Green has asked her research analyst, Ian Cook, for a valuation of each of these properties under the income, cost, and sales comparison approaches using the information provided in Exhibit 5 and the following two assumptions:

Assumption 1:   The holding period for each property is expected to be five years.

Assumption 2:   Property B is expected to have the same net operating income for the holding period because of existing leases and a one-time 20% increase in Year 6 because of lease rollovers. No further growth is assumed thereafter.

In reviewing Exhibit 5, Green notes the disproportionate estimated obsolescence charges for Property C relative to the other properties and asks Cook to verify the reasonableness of these estimates. Green also reminds Cook that they will need to conduct proper due diligence. In that regard, Green indicates that she is concerned whether a covered parking lot that was added to Property A encroaches (is partially located) on adjoining properties. Green would like for Cook to identify an expert and present documentation to address her concerns regarding the parking lot.

In addition to discussing the new allocation, the CIO informs Green that she wants to discuss the appropriate real estate index for the private equity real estate quadrant at the upcoming meeting. The CIO believes that the current index may result in over-allocating resources to the private equity real estate quadrant.

13. The *most* effective justification that Green could present for directing the increased allocation to her quadrant would be that relative to the other quadrants, her quadrant of real estate investments:
    A. provides greater liquidity.
    B. requires less professional management.
    C. enables greater decision-making control.

14. Relative to the expected correlation between First Life's portfolio of public REIT holdings and its stock and bond portfolio, the expected correlation between First Life's private equity real estate portfolio and its stock and bond portfolio is *most likely* to be:
    A. lower.
    B. higher.
    C. the same.

15. Which of the properties in Exhibit 5 exposes the owner to the greatest risk related to operating expenses?
    A. Property A
    B. Property B
    C. Property C

16. Which property in Exhibit 5 is *most likely* to be affected by import and export activity?
    A. Property A
    B. Property B
    C. Property C

17. Which property in Exhibit 5 would *most likely* require the greatest amount of active management?
    A. Property A
    B. Property B
    C. Property C

18. Which property in Exhibit 5 is *most likely* to have a percentage lease?
    A. Property A
    B. Property B
    C. Property C
19. The disproportionate charges for Property C noted by Green are *least likely* to explicitly factor into the estimate of property value using the:
    A. cost approach.
    B. income approach.
    C. sales comparison approach.
20. Based on Exhibit 5, which of the following statements regarding Property A is *most* accurate?
    A. The going-in capitalization rate is 13.5%.
    B. It appears to be the riskiest of the three properties.
    C. The net operating income in the first year is £298,000.
21. Based on Exhibit 5, the value of Property C using the direct capitalization method is *closest* to:
    A. £3,778,900.
    B. £4,786,700.
    C. £6,527,300.
22. Based on Exhibit 5 and Assumptions 1 and 2, the value of Property B using the discounted cash flow method, assuming a five-year holding period, is *closest* to:
    A. £4,708,700.
    B. £5,034,600.
    C. £5,050,900.
23. Which method under the income approach is *least likely* to provide a realistic valuation for Property B?
    A. Layer method
    B. Direct capitalization method
    C. Discounted cash flow method
24. Based on Exhibit 5, the value of Property A using the cost approach is *closest* to:
    A. £5,281,000.
    B. £6,531,000.
    C. £9,385,000.
25. Based on Exhibit 5, the value of Property B using the sales comparison approach is *closest* to:
    A. £4,781,000.
    B. £4,858,000.
    C. £6,110,000.
26. Which due diligence item would be *most* useful in addressing Green's concerns regarding Property A?
    A. Property survey
    B. Engineering inspection
    C. Environmental inspection
27. The real estate index currently being used by First Life to evaluate private equity real estate investments is *most likely:*
    A. an appraisal-based index.
    B. a transaction-based index.
    C. the NCREIF Property Index.

28. Based on Exhibit 5, the property expected to be most highly leveraged is:
   A. Property A.
   B. Property B.
   C. Property C.

The following information relates to Questions 29–34.

Hui Lin, CFA, is an investment manager looking to diversify his portfolio by adding equity real estate investments. Lin and his investment analyst, Maria Nowak, are discussing whether they should invest in publicly traded real estate investment trusts or public real estate operating companies. Nowak expresses a strong preference for investing in public REITs in taxable accounts.

Lin schedules a meeting to discuss this matter, and for the meeting, Lin asks Nowak to gather data on three specific REITs and come prepared to explain her preference for public REITs over public REOCs. At the meeting, Lin asks Nowak,

> *"Why do you prefer to invest in public REITs over public REOCs for taxable accounts?"*

Nowak provides Lin with an explanation for her preference of public REITs and provides Lin with data on the three REITs shown in Exhibits 6 and 7.

The meeting concludes with Lin directing Nowak to identify the key investment characteristics along with the principal risks of each REIT and to investigate the valuation of the three REITs. Specifically, Lin asks Nowak to value each REIT using four different methodologies:

Method 1: Net asset value
Method 2: Discounted cash flow valuation using a two-step dividend model
Method 3: Relative valuation using property subsector average P/FFO multiple
Method 4: Relative valuation using property subsector average P/AFFO multiple

EXHIBIT 6   Select REIT Financial Information

	REIT A	REIT B	REIT C
Property subsector	Office	Storage	Health Care
Estimated 12-month cash net operating income	$350,000	$267,000	$425,000
Funds from operations	$316,965	$290,612	$368,007
Cash and equivalents	$308,700	$230,850	$341,000
Accounts receivable	$205,800	$282,150	$279,000
Debt and other liabilities	$2,014,000	$2,013,500	$2,010,000
Non-cash rents	$25,991	$24,702	$29,808
Recurring maintenance-type capital expenditures	$63,769	$60,852	$80,961
Shares outstanding	56,100	67,900	72,300

EXHIBIT 7   REIT Dividend Forecasts and Average Price Multiples

	REIT A	REIT B	REIT C
Expected annual dividend next year	$3.80	$2.25	$4.00
Dividend growth rate in Years 2 and 3	4.0%	5.0%	4.5%
Dividend growth rate (after Year 3 into perpetuity)	3.5%	4.5%	4.0%
Assumed cap rate	7.0%	6.25%	6.5%
Property subsector average P/FFO multiple	14.4×	13.5×	15.1×
Property subsector average P/AFFO multiple	18.3×	17.1×	18.9×

Note: Nowak estimates an 8% cost of equity capital for all REITs and a risk-free rate of 4.0%.

29. Nowak's *most likely* response to Lin's question is that the type of real estate security she prefers:
    A. offers a high degree of operating flexibility.
    B. provides dividend income that is exempt from double taxation.
    C. has below-average correlations with overall stock market returns.
30. Based on Exhibits 6 and 7, the value per share for REIT A using valuation Method 1 is *closest* to:
    A. $51.26.
    B. $62.40.
    C. $98.30.
31. Based on Exhibits 6 and 7, the value per share of REIT B using valuation Method 3 is *closest* to:
    A. $40.77.
    B. $57.78.
    C. $73.19.
32. Based on Exhibit 7, the value per share of REIT C using valuation Method 2 is *closest* to:
    A. $55.83.
    B. $97.57.
    C. $100.91.
33. Based on Exhibits 6 and 7, the value per share of REIT A using valuation Method 4 is *closest* to:
    A. $58.32.
    B. $74.12.
    C. $103.40.
34. The risk factor *most likely* to adversely affect an investment in REIT B is:
    A. new competitive facilities.
    B. tenants' sales per square foot.
    C. obsolescence of existing space.

The following information relates to Questions 35–40.

Tim Wang is a financial adviser specializing in commercial real estate investing. He is meeting with Mark Caudill, a new client who is looking to diversify his investment portfolio by adding real estate investments. Caudill has heard about various investment vehicles related to real estate from his friends and is seeking a more in-depth understanding of these investments from Wang.

Wang begins the meeting by advising Caudill of the many options that are available when investing in real estate, including the following:

Option 1:   Direct ownership in real estate
Option 2:   Publicly traded real estate investment trusts
Option 3:   Publicly traded real estate operating companies
Option 4:   Publicly traded residential mortgage-backed securities

Wang next asks Caudill about his investment preferences. Caudill responds by telling Wang that he prefers to invest in equity securities that are highly liquid, provide high income, and are not subject to double taxation.

Caudill asks Wang how the economic performance of REITs and REOCs is evaluated and how their shares are valued. Wang advises Caudill there are multiple measures of economic performance for REITs and REOCs, including the following:

Measure 1:   Net operating income
Measure 2:   Funds from operations
Measure 3:   Adjusted funds from operations

In response, Caudill asks Wang,

> *"Which of the three measures is the best measure of a REIT's current economic return to shareholders?"*

To help Caudill's understanding of valuation, Wang presents Caudill with data on Baldwin, a health care REIT that primarily invests in independent and assisted senior housing communities in large cities across the United States. Selected financial data on Baldwin for the past two years are provided in Exhibit 8.

EXHIBIT 8   Baldwin REIT Summarized Income Statement (USD thousands, except per-share data)

	Year Ending 31 December	
	2019	2018
Rental income	339,009	296,777
Other property income	6,112	4,033
Total income	345,121	300,810
Rental expenses		
Property operating expenses	19,195	14,273
Property taxes	3,610	3,327
Total property expenses	22,805	17,600
Net operating income	322,316	283,210
Other income (gains on sale of properties)	2,162	1,003
General and administrative expenses	21,865	19,899

Depreciation and amortization	90,409	78,583
Net interest expenses	70,017	56,404
Net income	142,187	129,327
Weighted average shares outstanding	121,944	121,863
Earnings per share	1.17	1.06
Dividend per share	0.93	0.85
Price/FFO, based on year-end stock price	11.5×	12.7×

Before the meeting, Wang had put together some valuation assumptions for Baldwin in anticipation of discussing valuation with Caudill. Wang explains the process of valuing a REIT share using discounted cash flow analysis, and he proceeds to estimate the value of Baldwin on a per-share basis using a two-step dividend discount model using the data provided in Exhibit 9.

EXHIBIT 9   Baldwin Valuation Projections and Assumptions

Current risk-free rate	4.0%
Baldwin beta	0.90
Market risk premium	5.0%
Appropriate discount rate (CAPM)	8.5%
Expected dividend per share, 1 year from today	$1.00
Expected dividend per share, 2 years from today	$1.06
Long-term growth rate in dividends, starting in Year 3	5.0%

35. Based on Caudill's investment preferences, the type of real estate investment Wang is *most likely* to recommend to Caudill is:
    A. Option 2.
    B. Option 3.
    C. Option 4.
36. Relative to Option 2 and Option 3, an advantage of investing in Option 1 is:
    A. greater liquidity.
    B. lower investment requirements.
    C. greater control over property-level investment decisions.
37. The Baldwin REIT is *least likely* to experience long-run negative effects from:
    A. an economic recession.
    B. an unfavorable change in population demographics.
    C. a major reduction in government funding of health care.
38. The *most appropriate* response to Caudill's question is:
    A. Measure 1.
    B. Measure 2.
    C. Measure 3.

39. Based on Exhibit 8, the 2019 year-end share price of Baldwin was *closest* to:
    A. $13.23.
    B. $21.73.
    C. $30.36.

40. Based on Exhibit 9, the intrinsic value of the Baldwin REIT on a per share basis using the two-step dividend discount model is *closest* to:
    A. $26.72.
    B. $27.59.
    C. $28.76.

REAL ESTATE INVESTMENTS

SOLUTIONS

1. B is correct. The lease term for the anchor tenant is typically longer than the usual three- to five-year term for smaller tenants. The data in Exhibit P3.1 suggest that the operating expenses are passed on to the tenant; the sum of property management fees and other operating expenses equals the expense reimbursement revenue. Also, other income is only $15,000, suggesting that a minimal amount of percentage rent is linked to sales thresholds.

2. C is correct. The terminal value using the income approach is $53,632,650 (= Year 6 NOI/terminal cap rate = $3,217,959/0.06). The value of the property using the cost approach is $61 million (= Land value + Building replacement cost − Total depreciation = $7,000,000 + $59,000,000 − $5,000,000). The adjusted sales price per square foot for Sales Comp B is $462 psf (= $395 × 1.17).

3. C is correct. There is a constant growth rate in income and value: Growth rate = Discount rate (7.25%) − Going-in cap rate (5.25%) = 2.00%.

4. B is correct. The value of Property 1 using the discounted cash flow method is $49,750,931, or $49,750,900 rounded, calculated as follows:

		Discount Period	Discounted Value[a]
Year 1 NOI	$2,775,840	1	$2,588,196
Year 2 NOI	$2,859,119	2	$2,485,637
Year 3 NOI	$2,944,889	3	$2,387,135
Year 4 NOI	$3,033,235	4	$2,292,540
Year 5 NOI	$3,124,232	5	$2,201,693
Terminal Value[b]	$53,632,650	5	$37,795,731
Property 1 DCF Value			$49,750,932

[a]Discount rate = 7.25%.

[b]Terminal value = Year 6 NOI/Terminal cap rate = $3,217,959/0.06 = $53,632,650.

5. C is correct. The direct capitalization method estimate of value for Property 1 is $52,873,143 (= Year 1 NOI/Going-in cap rate = $2,775,840/0.0525), which is greater than the estimated DCF value of $49,750,932.

The value of Property 1 using the discounted cash flow method can be calculated from the following table:

		Discount Period	Discounted Value[a]
Year 1 NOI	$2,775,840	1	$2,588,196
Year 2 NOI	$2,859,119	2	$2,485,637
Year 3 NOI	$2,944,889	3	$2,387,135
Year 4 NOI	$3,033,235	4	$2,292,540
Year 5 NOI	$3,124,232	5	$2,201,693
Terminal Value[b]	$53,632,650	5	$37,795,731
Property 1 DCF Value			$49,750,932

[a]Discount rate = 7.25%.

[b]Terminal value = Year 6 NOI/Terminal cap rate = $3,217,959/0.06 = $53,632,650.

6. C is correct. The estimate of the value of Property 1 using the sales comparison approach can be calculated using the following table:

	Unadjusted psf	Adjusted psf
Sales Comp 1	$415	$394 (= $415 × 0.95)
Sales Comp 2	$395	$462 (= $395 × 1.17)
Sales Comp 3	$400	$480 (= $400 × 1.20)
Average	$403	$445

Estimated value of Property 1 = $44,500,000 (= $445 psf × 100,000 sf).

7. C is correct. The due diligence process includes a review of leases for major tenants, which would include the grocery anchor tenant. Typically, only major tenant leases will be reviewed in the due diligence process; smaller tenant leases will likely not be reviewed. Also, the fact that other income is only $15,000 suggests that percentage rent linked to sales levels is minimal and has not been underwritten in the valuation and acquisition process.

8. B is correct. Delphinus will expect to earn a higher return on equity with the use of a mortgage to finance a portion of the purchase. The quoted mortgage interest rate of 5.75% is less than the discount rate of 7.25%.

9. A is correct. The maximum amount of debt that an investor can obtain on commercial real estate is usually limited by either the ratio of the loan to the appraised value of the property (loan-to-value, or LTV, ratio) or the debt service coverage ratio (DSCR), depending on which measure results in the lowest loan amount. The maximum LTV ratio is 75% of the appraised value of $48 million, or $36,000,000. The loan amount based on the minimum DSCR would be $32,183,652, determined as follows:

Maximum debt service = Year 1 NOI/DSCR = $2,775,840/1.5 = $1,850,560.

Loan amount (interest-only loan) = Maximum debt service/Mortgage rate = $1,850,560/0.0575 = $32,183,652 (rounded to $32,000,000).

10. A is correct. Benefits of private equity real estate investments include the owners' ability to attain diversification benefits, to earn current income, and to achieve tax benefits.

11. A is correct. Business conditions, demographics, the cost of debt and equity capital, and financial leverage are characteristic sources of risk for real estate investments.

12. A is correct. Richmond Life's investment would be a mortgage that falls under private debt in the four quadrants.

13. C is correct. Private equity investments in real estate enable greater decision-making control relative to real estate investments in the other three quadrants. A private real estate equity investor or direct owner of real estate has responsibility for the management of the real estate, including maintaining the properties, negotiating leases, and collecting rents. These responsibilities increase the investor's control in the decision-making process. Investors in publicly traded REITs or real estate debt instruments would not typically have significant influence over these decisions.

14. A is correct. Evidence suggests that private equity real estate investments have a lower correlation with stocks and bonds than publicly traded REITs. When real estate is publicly traded, it tends to behave more like the rest of the stock market than the real estate market.

15. B is correct. Property B is a gross lease, which requires the owner to pay the operating expenses. Accordingly, the owner, First Life, incurs the risk of Property B's operating expenses, such as utilities, increasing in the future.

16. C is correct. Property C is a warehouse and is most likely affected by import and export activity in the economy. Property A (office) and Property B (retail) would typically be less dependent on import and export activity compared with a warehouse property.

17. B is correct. Property B is a shopping center and would most likely require more active management than a single-tenant office (Property A) or a warehouse (Property C); the owner would need to maintain the right tenant mix and promote the facility.

18. B is correct. Property B is a shopping center, a type of retail property. A percentage lease is a unique aspect of many retail leases, which requires the tenant to pay additional rent once its sales reach a certain level. The lease will typically specify a "minimum rent" that must be paid regardless of the tenant's sales. Percentage rent may be paid by the tenant once the tenant's sales reach a certain level or breakpoint.

19. B is correct. Obsolescence charges reduce the value of a property using the cost approach and are factored into the sales comparison approach by adjustments, including condition and location, to the price per square meter. The cash flows to the property should reflect obsolescence: Less rent is received if the property is not of an appropriate design for the intended use, if it is in a poor location, or if economic conditions are poor. Therefore, obsolescence is implicitly, not explicitly, factored into the estimate of property value using the income approach.

20. B is correct. Property A has been assigned the highest discount rate (11.5%) and thus is considered to be the riskiest investment of the three alternatives. This may be the result of the reliance on a single tenant. The going-in capitalization rate is 9.5% (Cap rate = Discount rate – Growth rate). The net operating income is £580,500 (= Rental income + Other income – Property management fee = £575,000 + £27,000 – £21,500).

21. C is correct. Under the direct capitalization method, the value of the property = NOI/$(r - g)$.

Calculate net operating income (NOI):

NOI = Rental income + Other income − Vacancy and collection loss − Property management costs.

NOI = £590,000 + £29,500 − £59,000 − £22,000 = £538,500.

Then, value the property using the cap rate:

Value of property = £538,500/(11.25% − 3.0%) = £6,527,273, rounded to £6,527,300.

22. B is correct. The value of Property B using the discounted cash flow method is £5,034,600. The value using the discounted cash flow method is based on the present value of the net operating income and the estimated property resale price.
    Calculate NOI (constant during the five-year holding period from Assumption 2):

NOI = Rental income (at full occupancy) + Other income − Vacancy and collection loss − Property management fee − Other operating expenses.

NOI = £610,000 + £183,000 − £61,000 − £35,000 − £234,000 = £463,000.
Estimate property value at the end of five years:

NOI starting in Year 6 is 20% higher because of lease rollovers (from Assumption 2).

NOI starting in Year 6 = £463,000 × 1.20 = £555,600.

Terminal cap rate (given) = 11%.

Applying the terminal cap rate yields a property value of £5,050,909 (= £555,600/0.11).

Find the present value of the expected annual NOI and the estimated property resale value using the given discount rate of 9.25%:

$$N = 5.$$

$$FV = £5,050,909.$$

$$PMT = £463,000.$$
$$I = 9.25.$$

Solving for PV, the current value of the property is estimated to be £5,034,643, or £5,034,600 rounded.

23. B is correct. The net operating income for Property B is expected to be level for the next five years, because of existing leases, and grow 20% in Year 6. A direct capitalization method would not be appropriate because of the multiple growth rates. A discounted cash flow method that assigns a terminal value, or a layer method, should be used.

24. A is correct. The value of Property A using the cost method is equal to the replacement cost, adjusted for the different types of depreciation (loss in value):

Value of Property A = Land value + (Replacement building cost + Developer's profit) − Deterioration − Functional obsolescence − Locational obsolescence − Economic obsolescence

= £1,500,000 + (£8,725,000 + £410,000) − £4,104,000 − £250,000 − £500,000 − £500,000

= £5,281,000.

25. B is correct. The value of a property using the sales comparison approach equals the adjusted price per square meter using comparable properties times property size. The value of Property B using the sales comparison approach is calculated as follows:

    Average adjusted price per square meter of Comparable Properties 1, 2, and 3 for Property B = (£950 + £1,090 + £875)/3 = £971.67.

    Applying the £971.67 average adjusted price per square meter to Property B gives a value of £4,858,300 (= £971.67 × 5,000 square meters = £4,858,350, or £4,858,000 rounded).

26. A is correct. A property survey can determine whether the physical improvements, such as the covered parking lot, are in the boundary lines of the site and whether any easements would affect the value of the property.

27. A is correct. An appraisal-based index is most likely to result in the over-allocation mentioned by the CIO due to the appraisal lag. The appraisal lag tends to "smooth" the index, meaning that it has less volatility. It behaves somewhat like a moving average of what an index would look like if it were based on values obtained from transactions rather than appraisals. Thus, appraisal-based indexes may underestimate the volatility of real estate returns. Because of the lag in the index, appraisal-based real estate indexes will also tend to have a lower correlation with other asset classes. This situation is problematic if the index is used in asset allocation models; the amount allocated to the asset class that appears to have lower correlation with other asset classes and less volatility will be greater than it should be.

28. C is correct. Property C has an expected loan-to-value ratio of 80%, which is higher than the loan-to-value ratio for Property A (70%) or Property B (75%).

29. B is correct. REITs are tax-advantaged entities, whereas REOC securities are not typically tax-advantaged entities. More specifically, REITs are typically exempt from the double taxation of income that comes from taxes being due at the corporate level and again when dividends or distributions are made to shareholders in some jurisdictions, such as the United States.

30. B is correct. The NAV is $62.40.

Estimated cash NOI	350,000
Assumed cap rate	0.07
Estimated value of operating real estate (350,000/0.07)	5,000,000
Plus: Cash + accounts receivable	514,500
Less: Debt and other liabilities	2,014,000
Net asset value	3,500,500
Shares outstanding	56,100
NAV/share	**$62.40**

31. B is correct. The value per share is $57.78, calculated as follows:

    Funds from operations = $290,612.
    Shares outstanding = 67,900 shares.
    FFO/share = $290,612/67,900 shares = $4.28.

    Applying the property subsector average P/FFO multiple of 13.5× yields a value per share of

    $$\$4.28 \times 13.5 = \$57.78.$$

32. C is correct. The value per share for REIT C is $100.91.

		Step 1		Step 2
	Year 1	Year 2	Year 3	Year 4
Dividends per share:	$4.00	$4.18	$4.37	$4.54
Value of stock at end of 2013:[a]			$113.57	
			$117.94	

Discount rate: 8.00%

Net present value of all dividends:[b] $100.91

[a]Calculated as $4.54/(0.08 − 0.04) = $113.57.

[b]Calculated as $4.00/(1.08) + $4.18/(1.08)^2 + $117.94/(1.08)^3 = $100.91.

33. B is correct. The value per share is $74.11, calculated as follows:

Funds from operations (FFO) = $316,965.
Less: Non-cash rents: $25,991
Less: Recurring maintenance-type capital expenditures: $63,769
Equals: AFFO: $227,205
Shares outstanding = 56,100 shares.
AFFO/share = $227,205/56,100 shares = $4.05.

Applying the property subsector average P/AFFO multiple of 18.3× yields a value per share of

$$\$4.05 \times 18.3 = \$74.12.$$

34. A is correct. As a storage REIT, this investment faces competitive pressures because the ease of entry into the field of self-storage properties can lead to periods of overbuilding.
35. A is correct. Option 2 (publicly traded REITs) best satisfies Caudill's investment preferences. REITs are equity investments that, in general, are income tax exempt at the corporate/trust level, so there is no double income taxation. To qualify for the income tax exemption, REITs are legally obligated to pay out a high percentage of income to their shareholders, which typically results in relatively high income for investors. Lastly, public REITs are generally liquid because they are traded in stock exchanges.
36. C is correct. Direct property ownership offers greater control over property-level investment decisions compared with the level of control exhibited by shareholders in REITs and REOCs.
37. A is correct. Baldwin, a health care REIT, is largely resistant to economic recessions but is exposed to changes in population demographics and changes in government funding for health care.
38. C is correct. Measure 3, adjusted funds from operations, is a refinement of FFO that is designed to be a more accurate measure of current economic income. In essence, FFO is adjusted to remove any non-cash rent and to include a provision for maintenance-type capital expenditures and leasing costs. Maintenance expenses are required for a business to continue as a going concern.

39. B is correct. Baldwin's FFO per share in 2019 was $1.89, and the resulting share price was $21.73. First, calculate FFO per share in 2019, and then apply the year-end P/FFO multiple of 11.5×.

    FFO = accounting net earnings, excluding (a) depreciation charges on real estate, (b) deferred tax charges, and (c) gains or losses from sales of property and debt restructuring.
    2019 accounting net income: $142,187
    2019 depreciation charges: $90,409
    2019 deferred tax charges: na
    2019 gains on sale of properties (other income): $2,162
    2019 shares outstanding: 121,944
    2019 year-end price/FFO = 11.5×.
    2019 Baldwin FFO per share = ($142,187 + $90,409 − $2,162)/121,944 shares = $1.89.
    At the given 2019 year-end price/FFO multiple of 11.5×, this results in a share price for Baldwin of $1.89 × 11.5 = $21.73.

40. C is correct. The estimated value per share for the Baldwin REIT using a two-step dividend discount model is $28.76, calculated as follows:

	Step 1		Step 2
	Year 1	Year 2	Year 3
Dividends per share:	$1.00	$1.06	$1.11
Value of stock at end of Year 2:[a]		$31.71	
		$32.77	

Discount rate: 8.50%

Net present value of all dividends:[b] $28.83

[a]Calculated as $1.11/(0.085 − 0.05) = $31.71.

[b]Calculated as $1.00/(1.085) + $32.77/(1.085)^2 = $28.76.

PRIVATE EQUITY INVESTMENTS

LEARNING OUTCOMES

The candidate should be able to:

- explain sources of value creation in private equity;
- explain how private equity firms align their interests with those of the managers of portfolio companies;
- compare and contrast characteristics of buyout and venture capital investments;
- interpret LBO model and VC method output;
- explain alternative exit routes in private equity and their impact on value;
- explain risks and costs of investing in private equity;
- explain private equity fund structures, terms, due diligence, and valuation in the context of an analysis of private equity fund returns;
- interpret and compare financial performance of private equity funds from the perspective of an investor;
- calculate management fees, carried interest, net asset value, distributed to paid in (DPI), residual value to paid in (RVPI), and total value to paid in (TVPI) of a private equity fund.

SUMMARY OVERVIEW

- Private equity funds seek to add value by various means, including optimizing financial structures, incentivizing management, and creating operational improvements.
- Private equity can be thought of as an alternative system of governance for corporations: Rather than ownership and control being separated as in most publicly quoted companies, private equity concentrates ownership and control. Many view the combination of

ownership and control as a fundamental source of the returns earned by the best private equity funds.

- A critical role for the GP is valuation of potential investments. But because these investments are usually privately owned, valuation encounters many challenges.
- Valuation techniques differ according to the nature of the investment. Early-stage ventures require very different techniques than leveraged buyouts. Private equity professionals tend to use multiple techniques when performing a valuation, and they explore many different scenarios for the future development of the business.
- In buyouts, the availability of debt financing can have a big impact on the scale of private equity activity, and it seems to impact valuations observed in the market.
- Because private equity funds are incentivized to acquire, add value, and then exit within the lifetime of the fund, they are considered buy-to-sell investors. Planning the exit route for the investment is a critical role for the GP, and a well-timed and well-executed investment can be a significant source of realized value.
- In addition to the problems encountered by the private equity funds in valuing potential portfolio investments, challenges exist in valuing the investment portfolio on an ongoing basis. This is because the investments have no easily observed market value and there is a large element of judgment involved in valuing each of the portfolio companies prior to their sale by the fund.
- The two main metrics for measuring the ongoing and ultimate performance of private equity funds are IRR and multiples. Comparisons of PE returns across funds and with other assets are demanding because it is important to control for the timing of cash flows, differences in risk and portfolio composition, and vintage-year effects.

PROBLEMS

1. Jo Ann Ng is a senior analyst at SING INVEST, a large regional mid-market buyout manager in Singapore. She is considering the exit possibilities for an existing investment in a mature automotive parts manufacturer that was acquired three years ago at a multiple of 7.5 times EBITDA. SING INVEST originally anticipated exiting its investment in China Auto Parts, Inc., within three to six years. Ng noted that market conditions have deteriorated and that companies operating in a similar business trade at an average multiple of 5.5 times EBITDA. She expects, however, based on analyst reports and industry knowledge, that the market will recover strongly within the next two years because of the fast-increasing demand for cars in emerging markets. Upon review of market opportunities, Ng also noted that China Gear Box, Inc., a smaller Chinese automotive parts manufacturer that presents strong potential synergies with China Auto Parts, Inc., is available for sale at an EBITDA multiple of 4.5. Exits by means of an IPO or a trade sale to a financial or strategic (company) buyer are possible in China. How would you advise Ng to enhance value upon exit of China Auto Parts?
2. Wenda Lee, CFA, is a portfolio manager at a UK-based private equity institutional investor. She is considering an investment in a mid-market European buyout fund to achieve better diversification for her firm's private equity portfolio. She short-listed two funds that she sees as having similar risk–return profiles. Before deciding which one to invest in, she is carefully reviewing and comparing the terms of each fund.

	Mid-market Fund A	Mid-market Fund B
Management fees	2.5%	1.5%
Transaction fees	100% to the GP	50–50% split
Carried interest	15%	20%
Hurdle rate	6%	9%
Clawback provision	No	Yes
Distribution waterfall	Deal by deal	Total return

Based on the analysis of terms, which fund would you recommend to Lee?

3. Jean-Pierre Dupont is the chief investment officer (CIO) of a French pension fund that allocates a substantial portion of its assets to private equity. The fund's PE portfolio comprises mainly large buyout funds and mezzanine funds with a limited allocation to a special situations fund. A decision has been made to increase allocations to European venture capital. The investment committee of the pension fund requested that Dupont present an analysis of five key investment characteristics specific to venture capital relative to buyout investing. Can you assist Dupont in this request?

4. Discuss the ways that private equity funds can create value.

5. What problems are encountered when using comparable publicly traded companies to value private acquisition targets?

6. What are the main ways that the performance of private equity limited partnerships can be measured (A) during the life of the fund and (B) once all investments have been exited?

The following information relates to Questions 7–12.

Martha Brady is the CIO of the Upper Darby County (UDC) public employees' pension system. Brady is considering an allocation of the pension system's assets to private equity. She has asked two of her analysts, Jennifer Chau, CFA, and Matthew Hermansky, to provide more information about the workings of the private equity market.

Brady recognizes that the private equity asset class covers a broad spectrum of equity investments that are not traded in public markets. She asks Chau to describe the major differences between assets within this asset class. Chau notes that private equity ranges from venture capital financing of early-stage companies to complete buyouts of large publicly traded or even privately held companies. Chau describes some of the characteristics of venture capital and buyout investments.

Chau mentions that private equity firms take care to align the economic interests of the managers of the investments they control with their own. Various contractual clauses are inserted in the compensation contracts of the management team in order to reward or punish managers who meet or do not meet agreed-upon target objectives.

One concern Chau highlights is the illiquidity of private equity investments over time. Some funds are returned to investors, however, over the life of the fund because a number of investment opportunities are exited early. Provisions in a fund's prospectus describe the distribution of returns to investors, some of which favor the limited partners. One such provision is the distribution waterfall mechanism that provides distributions to limited partners (LPs) before the general partner (GP) receives the carried interest. This distribution mechanism is called the total return waterfall.

Chau prepares the following data to illustrate the distribution waterfall mechanism and the funds provided to limited partners when a private equity fund with a zero hurdle rate exits from its first three projects during a three-year period.

EXHIBIT 1   Investment Returns and Distribution Waterfalls

Private equity committed capital	$400 million
Carried interest	20%
First project investment capital	$20 million
Second project investment capital	$45 million
Third project investment capital	$50 million
Proceeds from first project	$25 million
Proceeds from second project	$35 million
Proceeds from third project	$65 million

Chau cautions that investors must understand the terminology used to describe the performance of private equity funds. Interpretation of performance numbers should be made with the awareness that much of the fund assets are illiquid during a substantial part of the fund's life. She provides the latest data in Exhibit 2 for the Alpha, Beta, and Gamma Funds, diversified high-technology venture capital funds formed five years ago, each with five years remaining to termination.

EXHIBIT 2   Financial Performance of Alpha, Beta, and Gamma Funds

Fund	PIC	DPI	RVPI
Alpha	0.30	0.10	0.65
Beta	0.85	0.10	1.25
Gamma	0.85	1.25	0.75

Chau studies the data and comments that of the three funds, the Alpha Fund has the best chance to outperform over the remaining life. First, it's because the management has earned such a relatively high residual value on capital and will be able to earn a high return on the remaining funds called down. At termination, the RVPI will be double the 0.65 value when the rest of the funds are called down. Second, its cash-on-cash return as measured by DPI is already as high as that of the Beta Fund. The PIC (or paid-in capital) ratio indicates the proportion of capital already called by the GP. The PIC of Alpha is relatively low relative to Beta and Gamma.

Hermansky notes that a private equity fund's ability to properly plan and execute its exit from an investment is vital for the fund's success. Venture funds, such as Alpha, Beta, and Gamma, take special care to plan their exits.

Brady then asks the analysts what procedures private equity firms would use to value investments in their portfolios as well as investments that are added later. She is concerned about buying into a fund with existing assets that do not have public market prices that can be used to ascertain value. In such cases, she worries, what if a GP overvalues the assets and new investors in the fund pay more for the fund assets than they are worth?

Hermansky makes three statements regarding the valuation methods used in private equity transactions during the early stages of selling a fund to investors:

Statement 1:   For venture capital investment in the early stages of analysis, emphasis is placed on the discounted cash flow approach to valuation.

Statement 2:   For buyout investments, income-based approaches are used frequently as a primary method of valuation.

Statement 3:   If a comparable group of companies exist, multiples of revenues or earnings are used frequently to derive a value for venture capital investments.

7. The characteristic that is *most likely* common to both the venture capital and buyout private equity investment is:
   A. measurable and assessable risk.
   B. the extensive use of financial leverage.
   C. the strength of the individual track record and ability of members of management.

8. The contractual term enabling management of the private equity–controlled company to be rewarded with increased equity ownership as a result of meeting performance targets is called:
   A. a ratchet.
   B. the tag-along right.
   C. the clawback provision.

9. For the projects described in Exhibit 1, under a deal-by-deal method with a clawback provision and true-up every three years, the cumulative dollar amount the GP receives by the end of the three years is equal to:
   A. 1 million.
   B. 2 million.
   C. 3 million.

10. Are Chau's two reasons for interpreting Alpha Fund as the best-performing fund over the remaining life correct?
    A. No
    B. Yes
    C. The first reason is correct, but the second reason is incorrect.

11. The exit route for a venture capital investment is *least likely* to be in the form of a(n):
    A. initial public offering (IPO).
    B. sale to other venture funds targeting the same sector.
    C. buyout by the management of the venture investment.

12. Which statement by Hermansky is the *least* valid?
    A. Statement 1
    B. Statement 2
    C. Statement 3

The following information relates to questions 13–18.

Daniel Collin is a junior analyst at JRR Equity Partners (JRR), a private equity firm. Collin is assigned to work with Susan Tseng, a senior portfolio manager. Tseng and Collin meet to discuss existing and potential investments.

Tseng starts the meeting with a discussion of LBO firms and VC firms. Collin tells Tseng,

> *LBO firms tend to invest in companies with predictable cash flows and experienced management teams, whereas VC firms tend to invest in companies with high EBITDA or EBIT growth and where an exit is fairly predictable.*

Tseng and Collin next analyze a potential investment in the leveraged buyout of Stoneham Industries. Specifically, they assess the expected gain if they elect to purchase all of the preference shares and 90% of the common equity through the LBO. Details of the LBO include the following:

- The buyout requires an initial investment of $10 million.
- Financing for the deal includes $6 million in debt, $3.6 million in preference shares that promise a 15% annual return paid at exit, and $0.4 million in common equity.

The expected exit value in six years is $15 million, with an estimated reduction in debt of $2.8 million over the six years prior to exit.

Tseng and Collin next discuss JRR's investment in Venture Holdings, a private equity fund. Selected details on the Venture Holdings fund include the following:

- Total committed capital is $115 million.
- The distribution waterfall follows the deal-by-deal method, and carried interest is 20%.
- On its first exit event a few years ago, the fund generated a $10 million profit.

At the end of the most recent year, cumulative paid-in capital was $98 million, cumulative distributions paid out to LPs were $28 million, and the year-end NAV, before and after distributions, was $170.52 million and $131.42 million, respectively.
Tseng and Collin estimate that the fund's NAV before distributions will be $242.32 million at the end of next year.

Finally, Tseng and Collin evaluate two venture capital funds for potential investment: the Squire Fund and the Treble Fund. Both funds are in Year 7 of an estimated 10-year term. Selected data for the two funds are presented in Exhibit 3.

EXHIBIT 3   Selected Data for the Squire Fund and the Treble Fund

	Squire Fund	Treble Fund
DPI	0.11	0.55
RVPI	0.95	0.51
Gross IRR	−11%	10%
Net IRR	−20%	8%

After reviewing the performance data in Exhibit 3, Collin draws the following conclusions:

Conclusion 1:   The unrealized return on investment for the Squire Fund is greater than the unrealized return on investment for the Treble Fund.

Conclusion 2:   The TVPI for the Treble Fund is higher than the TVPI for the Squire Fund because the Treble Fund has a higher gross IRR.

13. Is Collin's statement about LBO firms and VC firms correct?
    A. Yes
    B. No, because he is wrong with respect to VC firms
    C. No, because he is wrong with respect to LBO firms

14. The multiple of expected proceeds at exit to invested funds for JRR's Stoneham LBO investment is *closest* to:
    A. 2.77.
    B. 2.89.
    C. 2.98.

15. The distribution available to the limited partners of the Venture Holdings fund from the first exit is *closest* to:
    A. $2 million.
    B. $8 million.
    C. $10 million.

16. At the end of the most recent year, the ratio of total value to paid-in capital (TVPI) for the Venture Holdings fund was *closest* to:
    A. 0.29.
    B. 1.34.
    C. 1.63.

17. Based on Tseng and Collin's estimate of NAV next year, the estimate of carried interest next year is *closest* to:
    A. $14.36 million.
    B. $22 million.
    C. $25.46 million.

18. Which of Collin's conclusions regarding the Squire Fund and the Treble Fund is correct?
    A. Only Conclusion 1
    B. Only Conclusion 2
    C. Both Conclusion 1 and Conclusion 2

PRIVATE EQUITY INVESTMENTS

SOLUTIONS

1. The exit strategies available to SING INVEST to divest their holding in China Auto Parts, Inc., will largely depend on the following two factors:

    *   Time remaining until the fund's term expires: If the time remaining is sufficiently long, the fund's manager has more flexibility to work out an exit at more favorable market circumstances and terms.
    *   Amount of undrawn commitments from LPs in the fund: If sufficient LP commitments can be drawn, the fund manager may take advantage of current investment opportunities at depressed market prices to enhance returns upon exit in a more favorable market environment.

    In the case of China Auto Parts, Inc., depending on an analysis of the factors discussed, Ng could offer an opinion to support the acquisition of China Gear Box, Inc., subject to an in-depth analysis of potential synergies with China Auto Parts, Inc. The objective here may thus be twofold: to benefit from short-term market conditions and to enhance the value of existing investments by reinforcing their market potential with a strategic merger.

2. Assuming that both funds have similar risk-return characteristics, a closer analysis of economic and corporate governance terms should be instrumental in determining which fund to select.

    In economic terms, Mid-Market Fund B has a higher carried interest than Mid-Market Fund A, but Mid-Market Fund B has a fee structure that is better aligned with the interests of LPs. A larger proportion of Mid-Market Fund B's fees (through the carried interest) will come from achieving successful exits, whereas Mid-Market Fund A will earn relatively larger fees on running the fund (management fees and transaction fees) without necessarily achieving high performance. In addition, the 9% hurdle rate of Mid-Market

Fund B is indicative of confidence in the fund manager's ability to achieve a minimum compounded 9% return to LPs for which no carried interest will be paid.

In corporate governance terms, Mid-Market Fund B is far better aligned with the interests of LPs as a result of a clawback provision and a more favorable distribution waterfall that will allow payment of carried interest on a total return basis instead of deal by deal.

The conclusion is that Mid-Market Fund B appears better aligned with the interests of LPs.

3.

Venture Capital	Buyout
Primarily equity funded. Use of leverage is rare and very limited.	Extensive use of leverage consisting of a large proportion of senior debt and a significant layer of junior and/or mezzanine debt.
Returns of investment portfolios are generally characterized by very high returns from a limited number of highly successful investments and a significant number of write-offs from low performing investments or failures.	Returns of investment portfolios are generally characterized by lower variance across returns from underlying investments. Bankruptcies are rare events.
Venture capital firm monitors achievement of milestones defined in business plan and growth management.	Buyout firm monitors cash flow management and strategic and business planning.
Expanding capital requirement if in the growth phase.	Low working capital requirement.
Assessment of risk is difficult because of new technologies, new markets, and lack of operating history.	Risk is measurable (e.g., mature businesses, long operating history, etc.).

4. The main ways that private equity funds can create value include the following:

- Operational improvements and clearly defined strategies: In the case of later-stage companies and buyouts, private equity owners can often create value by focusing the business on its most profitable opportunities and providing strategic direction for the business. In the case of venture capital deals, the private equity funds provide valuable business experience, mentor management, and offer access to their network of contacts and other portfolio companies.
- Creating incentives for managers and aligning their goals with the investors: This is often achieved by providing significant monetary rewards to management if the private equity fund secures a profitable exit. In the case of buyouts, the free cash flow available to management is minimized by taking on significant amounts of debt financing.
- Optimizing the financial structure of the company: In the case of buyouts, the use of debt can reduce the tax payments made by the company and also reduce the cost of capital. There may also be opportunities in certain market conditions to take advantage of any mispricing of risk by lenders, which can allow the private equity funds to take advantage of interest rates that do not fully reflect the risks being carried by the lenders. Many would point to various periods from 2015 to 2019 when government interest rates were low, debt spreads were tight, and/or lender covenants were loose as examples of such prevailing conditions.

5. There are many complexities in using comparable companies to value private targets, including the following:

- The lack of public comparison companies operating in the same business, facing the same risks, and at the same stage of development. It is often possible to identify "approximate" comparisons but very rare to find an exact match. It is essential, therefore, to use judgment when using comparison company information, rather than just taking the average multiples derived from a sample of disparate companies.
- Comparison companies may have different capital structures, so estimated beta coefficients and some financial ratios should be adjusted accordingly.
- Reported accounting numbers for earnings must be chosen carefully and adjusted for any exceptional items, atypical revenues, and costs in the reference year. Care must also be taken to decide which earnings figures to compare; the main choices are trailing earnings (the last 12 months), earnings from the last audited accounts, or prospective year-ahead earnings.

6. In the early years of a fund, all measures of return are of little relevance because fees drag down the reported returns and investments are initially valued at cost. This produces the J-curve effect. After a few years (or longer in the case of venture capital investments), performance measures become more meaningful, and the two main measures used by investors are IRR and return multiples (of the initial sum invested). During the life of the fund, it is necessary to value the non-exited investments and add them to the realized returns. The former inevitably involves an element of judgment on the part of the General Partner, especially when it is difficult to estimate the likely market value of the investment. Once all the investments have been exited, the multiples and IRR can be estimated easily, taking account of the exact timing of the cash flows into and out of the fund. The most relevant measures for investors are computed net of management fees and any carried interest earned by the general partner.

7. C is correct. Members of both the firm being bought out and the venture capital investment usually have strong individual management track records. Extensive financial leverage is common in buyouts but not venture capital investments, whereas measurable risk is more common in buyouts than in venture capital situations.

8. A is correct.

9. B is correct. On a cumulative basis for three years, the fund earns $10 million, of which $2 million goes to the GP. The $2 million earned by the GP corresponds to 20% of the difference between total three-year proceeds and three-year invested capital, or $0.2 \times [(25 + 35 + 65) - (20 + 45 + 50)]$.

10. A is correct. Chau misinterprets DPI, RVPI, and PIC. The returns earned to date are for each dollar of invested capital—that which has been drawn down—not total returns. Chau mistakenly believes (assuming the same management skill) the result for Alpha Fund at termination will be on the order of $3 \times 0.65 = 1.95$, instead of 0.65. In both cases, Alpha Fund has underperformed relative to the other two funds.

11. C is correct. Leverage needed to finance a management buyout is not readily available to firms with limited history.

12. A is correct. Statement 1 is the least likely to be valid.

13. B is correct. LBO firms generally invest in firms with a predictable cash flow pattern (EBITDA or EBIT growth) and experienced management teams. In contrast, venture

capital firms tend to invest in new firms and new technologies with high revenue growth. Also, VC investments tend to be characterized as having exits that are difficult to anticipate.

14. B is correct. The investment exit value is $15 million. The expected payoff to JRR is calculated as follows (all amounts in millions):

Expected exit value:	$15.00
Debt remaining at exit: ($6.0 − 2.8)	3.20
Preference shares: [$3.60 × $(1.15)^6$]	8.33
Common equity: ($15 exit − 3.2 debt − 8.33 preference)	3.47

Initial investment: $3.6 (preference) + 0.9 × $0.4 (common) = $3.96.
Proceeds at exit: $8.33 (preference) + 0.9 × $3.47 (common) = $11.45.
Multiple of expected proceeds to invested funds: $11.45 exit value/$3.96 initial investment = 2.89×.

15. B is correct. The distribution waterfall for the Venture Holdings fund follows the deal-by-deal method. The investment generated a profit of $10 million, and with carried interest of 20%, the general partner would receive $2 million ($10 million × 20%), leaving $8 million for the limited partners.

16. C is correct. Total value to paid-in capital (TVPI) represents the fund's distributed value and undistributed value as a proportion of the cumulative invested capital. TVPI is the sum of distributed to paid-in capital (DPI) and residual value to paid-in capital (RVPI):

$$\text{DPI} = \frac{\text{Cumulative distributions}}{\text{Cumulative invested capital}} = \frac{\$28 \text{ million}}{\$98 \text{ million}} = 0.29\times$$

$$\text{RVPI} = \frac{\text{NAV (after distributions)}}{\text{Cumulative invested capital}} = \frac{\$131.42 \text{ million}}{\$98 \text{ million}} = 1.34\times$$

$$\text{TVPI} = \frac{\text{Cumulative distribution + NAV (after distributions)}}{\text{Cumulative invested capital}}$$

$$= \frac{\$28 \text{ million} + 131.42 \text{ million}}{\$98 \text{ million}} = 1.63\times$$

17. A is correct. Provided that NAV before distribution exceeds committed capital, the general partner is entitled to carried interest, calculated as the 20% multiplied by the increase in NAV before distributions. So, the carried interest is calculated as follows:

Carried interest = 20% × ($242.32 − $170.52) = $14.36 million.

18. A is correct. DPI provides an indication of a fund's realized return, whereas RVPI provides an indication of a fund's unrealized return. The Squire Fund has a higher RVPI (0.95) than the Treble Fund (0.51). TVPI, which is the sum of DPI and RVPI, is the same for both funds: 0.11 + 0.95 = 1.06 for the Squire Fund and 0.55 + 0.51 = 1.06 for the Treble Fund.

INTRODUCTION TO COMMODITIES AND COMMODITY DERIVATIVES

LEARNING OUTCOMES

The candidate should be able to:

- compare characteristics of commodity sectors;
- compare the life cycle of commodity sectors from production through trading or consumption;
- contrast the valuation of commodities with the valuation of equities and bonds;
- describe types of participants in commodity futures markets;
- analyze the relationship between spot prices and futures prices in markets in contango and markets in backwardation;
- compare theories of commodity futures returns;
- describe, calculate, and interpret the components of total return for a fully collateralized commodity futures contract;
- contrast roll return in markets in contango and markets in backwardation;
- describe how commodity swaps are used to obtain or modify exposure to commodities;
- describe how the construction of commodity indexes affects index returns.

SUMMARY OVERVIEW

- Commodities are a diverse asset class comprising various sectors: energy, grains, industrial (base) metals, livestock, precious metals, and softs (cash crops). Each of these sectors has a number of characteristics that are important in determining the supply and demand for each commodity, including ease of storage, geopolitics, and weather.
- Fundamental analysis of commodities relies on analyzing supply and demand for each of the products as well as estimating the reaction to the inevitable shocks to their equilibrium or underlying direction.
- The life cycle of commodities varies considerably depending on the economic, technical, and structural (i.e., industry, value chain) profile of each commodity as well as the sector. A short life cycle allows for relatively rapid adjustment to outside events, whereas a long life cycle generally limits the ability of the market to react.
- The valuation of commodities relative to that of equities and bonds can be summarized by noting that equities and bonds represent financial assets whereas commodities are physical assets. The valuation of commodities is not based on the estimation of future profitability and cash flows but rather on a discounted forecast of future possible prices based on such factors as the supply and demand of the physical item.
- The commodity trading environment is similar to other asset classes, with three types of trading participants: (1) informed investors/hedgers, (2) speculators, and (3) arbitrageurs.
- Commodities have two general pricing forms: spot prices in the physical markets and futures prices for later delivery. The spot price is the current price to deliver or purchase a physical commodity at a specific location. A futures price is an exchange-based price agreed on to deliver or receive a defined quantity and often quality of a commodity at a future date.
- The difference between spot and futures prices is generally called the basis. When the spot price is higher than the futures price, it is called backwardation, and when it is lower, it is called contango. Backwardation and contango are also used to describe the relationship between two futures contracts of the same commodity.
- Commodity contracts can be settled by either cash or physical delivery.
- There are three primary theories of futures returns.
  - In insurance theory, commodity producers who are long the physical good are motived to sell the commodity for future delivery to hedge their production price risk exposure.
  - The hedging pressure hypothesis describes when producers along with consumers seek to protect themselves from commodity market price volatility by entering into price hedges to stabilize their projected profits and cash flow.
  - The theory of storage focuses on supply and demand dynamics of commodity inventories, including the concept of "convenience yield."
- The total return of a fully collateralized commodity futures contract can be quantified as the spot price return plus the roll return plus the collateral return (risk-free rate return).
- The roll return is effectively the weighted accounting difference (in percentage terms) between the near-term commodity futures contract price and the farther-term commodity futures contract price.
- A commodity swap is a legal contract between two parties calling for the exchange of payments over multiple dates as determined by several reference prices or indexes.
- The most relevant commodity swaps include excess return swaps, total return swaps, basis swaps, and variance/volatility swaps.

- The five primary commodity indexes based on assets are: (1) the S&P GSCI; (2) the Bloomberg Commodity Index, formerly the Dow Jones–UBS Commodity Index; (3) the Deutsche Bank Liquid Commodity Index; (4) the Thomson Reuters/CoreCommodity CRB Index; and (5) the Rogers International Commodities Index.
- The key differentiating characteristics of commodity indexes are:
  - the breadth and selection methodology of coverage (number of commodities and sectors) included in each index, noting that some commodities have multiple reference contracts,
  - the relative weightings assigned to each component/commodity and the related methodology for how these weights are determined,
  - the methodology and frequency for rolling the individual futures contracts,
  - the methodology and frequency for rebalancing the weights of the individual commodities and sectors, and
  - the governance that determines which commodities are selected.

PROBLEMS

The following information relates to Questions 1–8.

Raffi Musicale is the portfolio manager for a defined benefit pension plan. He meets with Jenny Brown, market strategist with Menlo Bank, to discuss possible investment opportunities. The investment committee for the pension plan has recently approved expanding the plan's permitted asset mix to include alternative asset classes.

Brown proposes the Apex Commodity Fund (Apex Fund) offered by Menlo Bank as a potentially suitable investment for the pension plan. The Apex Fund attempts to produce trading profits by capitalizing on the mispricing between the spot and futures prices of commodities. The fund has access to storage facilities, allowing it to take delivery of commodities when necessary. The Apex Fund's current asset allocation is presented in Exhibit 1.

EXHIBIT 1   Apex Fund's Asset Allocation

Commodity Sector	Allocation (%)
Energy	31.9
Livestock	12.6
Softs	21.7
Precious metals	33.8

Brown explains that the Apex Fund has had historically low correlations with stocks and bonds, resulting in diversification benefits. Musicale asks Brown, "Can you identify a factor that affects the valuation of financial assets like stocks and bonds but does not affect the valuation of commodities?"

Brown shares selected futures contract data for three markets in which the Apex Fund invests. The futures data are presented in Exhibit 2.

EXHIBIT 2   Selected Commodity Futures Data*

Month	Gold Price	Coffee Price	Gasoline Price
July	1,301.2	0.9600	2.2701
September	1,301.2	0.9795	2.2076
December	1,301.2	1.0055	2.0307

* Gold: US$/troy ounce; coffee: US$/pound; gasoline: US$/gallon.

Menlo Bank recently released a report on the coffee market. Brown shares the key conclusion from the report with Musicale: "The coffee market had a global harvest that was greater than expected. Despite the large harvest, coffee futures trading activity is balanced between producers and consumers. This balanced condition is not expected to change over the next year."

Brown shows Musicale the total return of a recent trade executed by the Apex Fund. Brown explains that the Apex Fund took a fully collateralized long futures position in nearby soybean futures contracts at the quoted futures price of 865.0 (US cents/bushel). Three months later, the entire futures position was rolled when the near-term futures price was 877.0 and the farther-term futures price was 883.0. During the three-month period between the time that the initial long position was taken and the rolling of the contract, the collateral earned an annualized rate of 0.60%.

Brown tells Musicale that the pension fund could alternatively gain long exposure to commodities using the swap market. Brown and Musicale analyze the performance of a long position in an S&P GSCI total return swap having monthly resets and a notional amount of $25 million. Selected data on the S&P GSCI are presented in Exhibit 3.

EXHIBIT 3   Selected S&P GSCI Data

Reference Date	Index Level
April (swap initiation)	2,542.35
May	2,582.23
June	2,525.21

1. The Apex Fund is *most likely* to be characterized as:
   A. a hedger.
   B. a speculator.
   C. an arbitrageur.
2. Which factor would *most likely* affect the supply or demand of all four sectors of the Apex Fund?
   A. Weather
   B. Spoilage
   C. Government actions
3. The *most appropriate* response to Musicale's question regarding the valuation factor is:
   A. storage costs.
   B. transportation costs.
   C. expected future cash flows.

4. Which futures market in Exhibit 2 is in backwardation?
   A. Gold
   B. Coffee
   C. Gasoline
5. Based on the key conclusion from the Menlo Bank coffee market report, the shape of the coffee futures curve in Exhibit 2 is *most consistent* with the:
   A. insurance theory.
   B. theory of storage.
   C. hedging pressure hypothesis.
6. Based on Exhibit 2, which commodity's roll returns will *most likely* be positive?
   A. Gold
   B. Coffee
   C. Gasoline
7. The Apex Fund's three-month total return on the soybean futures trade is *closest* to:
   A. 0.85%.
   B. 1.30%.
   C. 2.22%.
8. Based on Exhibit 3, on the June settlement date, the party that is long the S&P GSCI total return swap will:
   A. owe a payment of $552,042.23.
   B. receive a payment of $1,502,621.33.
   C. receive a payment of $1,971,173.60.

The following information relates to Questions 9–15.

Jamal Nabli is a portfolio manager at NextWave Commodities (NWC), a commodity-based hedge fund located in the United States. NWC's strategy uses a fixed-weighting scheme to allocate exposure among 12 commodities, and it is benchmarked against the Thomson Reuters/ CoreCommodity CRB Index (TR/CC CRB). Nabli manages the energy and livestock sectors with the help of Sota Yamata, a junior analyst.

Nabli and Yamata meet to discuss a variety of factors that affect commodity values in the two sectors they manage. Yamata tells Nabli the following:

Statement 1: Storage costs are negatively related to futures prices.
Statement 2: In contrast to stocks and bonds, most commodity investments are made by using derivatives.
Statement 3: Commodities generate future cash flows beyond what can be realized through their purchase and sale.

Nabli and Yamata then discuss potential new investments in the energy sector. They review Brent crude oil futures data, which are presented in Exhibit 4.

EXHIBIT 4   Selected Data on Brent Crude Oil Futures

Spot Price	Near-Term Futures Price	Longer-Term Futures Price
77.56	73.64	73.59

Yamata presents his research related to the energy sector, which has the following conclusions:

- Consumers have been more concerned about prices than producers have.
- Energy is consumed on a real-time basis and requires minimal storage.

After concluding the discussion of the energy sector, Nabli reviews the performance of NWC's long position in lean hog futures contracts. Nabli notes that the portfolio earned a −12% price return on the lean hog futures position last year and a −24% roll return after the contracts were rolled forward. The position was held with collateral equal to 100% of the position at a risk-free rate of 1.2% per year.

Yamata asks Nabli to clarify how the state of the futures market affects roll returns. Nabli responds as follows:

> **Statement 4:** Roll returns are generally negative when a futures market is in contango.
>
> **Statement 5:** Roll returns are generally positive when a futures market is in backwardation.

As part of their expansion into new markets, NWC is considering changing its benchmark index. Nabli investigates two indexes as a possible replacement. These indexes both use similar weighting and rebalancing schemes. Index A includes contracts of commodities typically in contango, whereas Index B includes contracts of commodities typically in backwardation. Nabli asks Yamata how the two indexes perform relative to each other in a market that is trending upward.

Because of a substantial decline in drilling activity in the North Sea, Nabli believes the price of Brent crude oil will increase more than that of heavy crude oil. The actual price volatility of Brent crude oil has been lower than its expected volatility, and Nabli expects this trend to continue. Nabli also expects the level of the ICE Brent Index to increase from its current level. Nabli and Yamata discuss how to use swaps to take advantage of Nabli's expectations. The possible positions are: (1) a basis swap long on Brent crude oil and short on heavy crude oil, (2) a long volatility swap on Brent crude oil, and (3) a short position in an excess return swap that is based on a fixed level (i.e., the current level) of the ICE Brent Index.

9. Which of Nabli's statements regarding the valuation and storage of commodities is correct?
   A. Statement 1
   B. Statement 2
   C. Statement 3
10. Based on Exhibit 1, Yamata should conclude that the:
    A. calendar spread for Brent crude oil is $3.97.
    B. Brent crude oil futures market is in backwardation.
    C. basis for the near-term Brent crude oil futures contract is $0.05 per barrel.
11. Based on Exhibit 1 and Yamata's research on the energy sector, the shape of the futures price curve for Brent crude oil is most consistent with the:
    A. insurance theory.
    B. theory of storage.
    C. hedging pressure hypothesis.

12. The total return (annualized excluding leverage) on the lean hog futures contract is:
    A. −37.2%.
    B. −36.0%.
    C. −34.8%.

13. Which of Nabli's statements about roll returns is correct?
    A. Only Statement 4
    B. Only Statement 5
    C. Both Statement 4 and Statement 5

14. The *best* response to Nabli's question about the relative performance of the two indexes is that Index B is *most likely* to exhibit returns that are:
    A. lower than those of Index A.
    B. the same as those of Index A.
    C. higher than those of index A.

15. Given Nabli's expectations for crude oil, the *most appropriate* swap position is the:
    A. basis swap.
    B. volatility swap.
    C. excess return swap.

The following information relates to Questions 16–22.

Mary McNeil is the corporate treasurer at Farmhouse, which owns and operates several farms and ethanol production plants in the United States. McNeil's primary responsibility is risk management. Katrina Falk, a recently hired junior analyst at Farmhouse, works for McNeil in managing the risk of the firm's commodity price exposures. Farmhouse's risk management policy requires the use of futures to protect revenue from price volatility, regardless of forecasts of future prices, and prohibits risk managers from taking speculative positions.

McNeil meets with Falk to discuss recent developments in two of Farmhouse's commodity markets, grains and livestock. McNeil asks Falk about key characteristics of the two markets that affect revenues and costs. Falk tells McNeil the following:

Statement 1: The life cycle for livestock depends on the product and varies widely by product.

Statement 2: Grains have uniform, well-defined seasons and growth cycles specific to geographic regions.

A material portion of Farmhouse's revenue comes from livestock exports, and a major input cost is the cost of grains imported from outside the United States. Falk and McNeil next discuss three conclusions that Falk reached in an analysis of the grains and livestock markets:

Conclusion 1: Assuming demand for grains remains constant, extreme heat in the regions from which we import our grains will result in a benefit to us in the form of lower grain prices.

Conclusion 2: New tariffs on cattle introduced in our primary export markets will likely result in higher prices for our livestock products in our local market.

Conclusion 3: Major improvements in freezing technology allowing for longer storage will let us better manage the volatility in the prices of our livestock products.

McNeil asks Falk to gather spot and futures price data on live cattle, wheat, and soybeans, which are presented in Exhibit 5. Additionally, she observes that: (1) the convenience yield of soybeans exceeds the costs of its direct storage and (2) commodity producers as a group are less interested in hedging in the forward market than commodity consumers are.

EXHIBIT 5   Selected Commodity Price Data*

Market	Live Cattle Price	Wheat Price	Soybeans Price
Spot	109	407	846
Futures	108	407	850

* Live cattle: US cents per pound; wheat and soybeans: US cents per bushel.

A key input cost for Farmhouse in producing ethanol is natural gas. McNeil uses positions in natural gas (NG) futures contracts to manage the risk of natural gas price volatility. Three months ago, she entered into a long position in natural gas futures at a futures price of $2.93 per million British thermal units (MMBtu). The current price of the same contract is $2.99. Exhibit 6 presents additional data about the three-month futures position.

EXHIBIT 6   Selected Information—Natural Gas Futures Three-Month Position*

			Prices	
Commodity	Total Current $ Exposure	Position	Near-Term Futures (Current Price)	Farther-Term Futures
Natural Gas (NG)	5,860,000	Long	2.99	3.03

*NG: $ per MMBtu; 1 contract = 10,000 MMBtu.

The futures position is fully collateralized earning a 3% rate. McNeil decides to roll forward her current exposure in the natural gas position.

Each month, McNeil reports the performance of the energy futures positions, including details on price returns, roll returns, and collateral returns, to the firm's executive committee. A new committee member is concerned about the negative roll returns on some of the positions. In a memo to McNeil, the committee member asks her to explain why she is not avoiding positions with negative roll returns.

16. With respect to its risk management policy, Farmhouse can be *best* described as:
    A. a trader.
    B. a hedger.
    C. an arbitrageur.
17. Which of Falk's statements regarding the characteristics of the grains and livestock markets is correct?
    A. Only Statement 1
    B. Only Statement 2
    C. Both Statement 1 and Statement 2
18. Which of Falk's conclusions regarding commodity markets is correct?
    A. Conclusion 1
    B. Conclusion 2
    C. Conclusion 3

19. Which commodity market in Exhibit 5 is currently in a state of contango?
    A. Wheat
    B. Soybeans
    C. Live cattle
20. Based on Exhibit 5 and McNeil's two observations, the futures price of soybeans is *most* consistent with the:
    A. insurance theory.
    B. theory of storage.
    C. hedging pressure hypothesis.
21. Based on Exhibit 6, the total return from the long position in natural gas futures is *closest* to:
    A. 1.46%.
    B. 3.71%.
    C. 4.14%.
22. The *most appropriate* response to the new committee member's question is that:
    A. roll returns are negatively correlated with price returns.
    B. such roll returns are the result of futures markets in backwardation.
    C. such positions may outperform other positions that have positive roll returns.

INTRODUCTION TO COMMODITIES AND COMMODITY DERIVATIVES

SOLUTIONS

1. C is correct. Commodity arbitrage involves an ability to inventory physical commodities and the attempt to capitalize on mispricing between the commodity (along with related storage and financing costs) and the futures price. The Apex Fund has access to storage facilities and uses these facilities in the attempt to capitalize on mispricing opportunities.

2. C is correct. Government actions can affect the supply or demand of all four sectors of the Apex Fund. With respect to energy, environmental mandates imposed by governments have tightened pollution standards, which have led to increasing processing costs that negatively affect demand. The supply of livestock, such as hogs and cattle, is affected by government-permitted use of drugs and growth hormones. Softs, or cash crops, can be affected by government actions, such as the attempt to maintain strategic stockpiles to control domestic prices. The level of demand and relative value of a precious metal, such as gold, is directly linked to government actions associated with managing to inflation targets.

3. C is correct. Expected future cash flows affect the valuation of financial assets, such as stocks and bonds, but do not affect the valuation of commodities. Financial assets (stocks and bonds) are valued based on expected future cash flows. In contrast, the valuation of a commodity is based on a discounted forecast of a future commodity price, which incorporates storage and transportation costs.

4. C is correct. When the near-term (i.e., closer to expiration) futures contract price is higher than the longer-term futures contract price, the futures market for the commodity is in backwardation. Because gasoline is the only one of the three futures markets in Exhibit P5.2 in which the near-term futures contract price ($2.2701) is higher than the longer-term contract price ($2.0307), the gasoline futures market is the only one in backwardation.

5. B is correct. The theory of storage focuses on the level of commodity inventories and the state of supply and demand. A commodity that is regularly stored should have a higher

price in the future (contango) to account for those storage costs. Because coffee is a commodity that requires storage, its higher future price is consistent with the theory of storage.

6. C is correct. Roll returns are generally positive (negative) when the futures market is in backwardation (contango) and zero when the futures market is flat. Because the gasoline market is in backwardation, its roll returns will most likely be positive.

7. A is correct. The total return on the trade represents the sum of three components: price return, roll return, and collateral return.

$$\text{Price return} = (\text{Current price} - \text{Previous price})/\text{Previous price}$$
$$= (877.0 - 865.0)/865.0 = 1.387\%.$$

Roll return = [(Near-term futures contract closing price − Farther-term futures contract closing price)/Near-term futures contract closing price] × Percentage of the position in the futures contract being rolled.

Because the entire position is being rolled, the percentage of the position in the futures contract being rolled is equal to 100%. So:

$$\text{Roll return} = [(877.0 - 883.0)/877.0] \times 100\% = -0.684\%.$$
$$\text{Collateral return} = [3 \text{ months}/12 \text{ months}] \times 0.60\% = 0.15\%.$$
$$\text{Total return} = 1.387\% - 0.684\% + 0.15\% = 0.853\%.$$

8. A is correct. The total return swap involves a monthly cash settlement (reset) based on the performance of the underlying reference asset (S&P GSCI) given a notional amount of $25 million. If the level of the index increases between the two valuation dates (in this case, May and June), the long position (the swap buyer) receives payment. If the level of the index decreases between the two valuation dates, the swap seller receives payment.

   The return on the reference index for the month of June is $[(2,525.21 - 2,582.23)/2,582.23]$, which is equivalent to −2.2082%. Therefore, the swap buyer (long position) must pay the swap seller a cash settlement for the month of June. The June payment calculation is equal to $25,000,000 × −2.2082%, or −$552,042.23.

9. B is correct. The most common way to invest in commodities is via derivatives, and commodities do not generate future cash flows beyond what can be realized through their purchase and sale. Also, storage costs are positively related to futures prices. Physical assets have to be stored, and storage incurs costs (rent, insurance, spoilage, etc.). Therefore, a commodity that is regularly stored should have a higher price in the future to account for those storage costs.

10. B is correct. The Brent crude oil futures market is in a state of backwardation. Commodity futures markets are in a state of backwardation when the spot price is greater than the price of near-term (i.e., nearest-to-expiration) futures contracts and, correspondingly, the price of near-term futures contracts is greater than that of longer-term contracts. The calendar spread is the difference between the near-term futures contract price and the longer-term futures contract price, which is $73.64 – $73.59 = $0.05. The basis for the near-term Brent crude oil futures contract is the difference between the spot price and the near-term futures price: $77.56 – $73.59 = $3.97.

11. B is correct. The Brent crude oil futures market is in a state of backwardation. The spot price is greater than the price of near-term (i.e., nearest-to-expiration) futures contracts. Commodities (in this case, Brent crude oil) are physical assets, not virtual assets, such

as stocks and bonds. Physical assets have to be stored, and storage incurs costs (rent, insurance, inspections, spoilage, etc.). According to the theory of storage, a commodity that is consumed along a value chain that allows for just-in-time delivery and use (i.e., minimal inventories and storage) can avoid these costs. Yamata's research concluded that energy is consumed on a real-time basis and requires minimal storage. In this situation, demand dominates supply, and current prices are higher than futures prices (state of backwardation).

12. C is correct. The contract was held for one year, so the price return of –12% is an annualized figure. Additionally, the –24% roll return is also annualized. Nabli's collateral return equals 1.2% per year × 100% initial collateral investment = 1.2%. Therefore, the total return (annualized) is calculated as follows:

$$\text{Total return} = \text{Price return} + \text{Roll return} + \text{Collateral return}.$$
$$\text{Total return} = -12\% + (-24\%) + 1.2\% = -34.8\%.$$

13. C is correct. Roll returns are generally negative (positive) when the futures market is in contango (backwardation) and zero when the futures market is flat.

14. C is correct. Index B is likely to have higher performance than Index A in a market that is trending upward. Indexes that (perhaps inadvertently) contain contracts that more commonly trade in backwardation may improve forward-looking performance because this generates a positive roll return. Similarly, indexes that contain contracts that more commonly trade in contango may hurt performance for the same reason (i.e., negative roll return).

15. A is correct. Nabli expects the price of Brent crude oil to increase more than that of heavy crude oil, and Nabli can take advantage of this prediction by entering into a basis swap that is long Brent crude oil and short heavy crude oil. Nabli should take a short (not long) position in a volatility swap to take advantage of his prediction that Brent crude oil's price volatility will be lower than its expected volatility. Nabli should take a long (not short) position in an excess return swap to take advantage of his expectation that the level of the ICE Brent Index will increase faster than leading oil benchmarks.

16. B is correct. Hedgers trade in the futures markets to hedge their exposures related to the commodity, as stated in Farmhouse's risk management policy.

17. C is correct. The life cycle of livestock does vary widely by product. Grains have uniform, well-defined seasons and growth cycles specific to geographic regions. Therefore, both statements are correct.

18. C is correct. Commodity prices are affected by supply and demand, and improvements in freezing technology can improve the firm's ability to store its products for longer periods and manage the volatility of supply and demand. For example, during times of excess supply, a livestock producer, such as Farmhouse, can freeze its products and offer them during better market supply conditions.

19. B is correct. The futures market for soybeans is in a state of contango because the spot price is lower than the futures price.

20. C is correct. In Exhibit P5.5, the spot price of soybeans is less than the futures price. This observation can be explained only by the hedging pressure hypothesis. According to this hypothesis, hedging pressure occurs when both producers and consumers seek to protect themselves from commodity market price volatility by entering into price hedges to stabilize their projected profits and cash flows. If consumers are more interested in hedging than producers are, the futures price will exceed the spot price.

In contrast, the insurance theory predicts that the futures price has to be lower than the current spot price as a form of payment or remuneration to the speculator who takes on the price risk and provides price insurance to the commodity seller. Similarly, the theory of storage also predicts that when a commodity's convenience yield is greater than its direct storage costs, the futures price will be lower than the spot price.

21. A is correct. The total return for a fully collateralized position is the sum of the price return, the roll return, and the collateral return:

$$\text{Price return} = (\text{Current price} - \text{Previous price})/\text{Previous price}$$
$$= (2.99 - 2.93)/2.93$$
$$= 2.05\%.$$

$$\text{Roll return} = (\text{Near-term futures closing price} - \text{Farther-term futures}$$
$$\text{closing price})/\text{Near-term futures closing price} \times \text{Percentage of}$$
$$\text{position in futures contract being rolled}$$
$$= [(2.99 - 3.03)/2.99] \times 100\%$$
$$= -1.34\%.$$

$$\text{Collateral return} = \text{Annual rate} \times \text{Period length as a fraction of the year}$$
$$= 3\% \times 0.25$$
$$= 0.75\%.$$

Therefore, the total return for three months = 2.05% − 1.34% + 0.75% = 1.46%.

22. C is correct. Investment positions are evaluated on the basis of total return, and the roll return is part of the total return. Even though negative roll return negatively affects the total return, this effect could be more than offset by positive price and collateral returns. Therefore, it is possible that positions with negative roll returns outperform positions with positive roll returns, depending on the price and collateral returns.

HEDGE FUND STRATEGIES

LEARNING OUTCOMES

The candidate should be able to:

- discuss how hedge fund strategies may be classified;
- discuss investment characteristics, strategy implementation, and role in a portfolio of *equity-related* hedge fund strategies;
- discuss investment characteristics, strategy implementation, and role in a portfolio of *event-driven* hedge fund strategies;
- discuss investment characteristics, strategy implementation, and role in a portfolio of *relative value* hedge fund strategies;
- discuss investment characteristics, strategy implementation, and role in a portfolio of *opportunistic* hedge fund strategies;
- discuss investment characteristics, strategy implementation, and role in a portfolio of *specialist* hedge fund strategies;
- discuss investment characteristics, strategy implementation, and role in a portfolio of *multi-manager* hedge fund strategies;
- describe how factor models may be used to understand hedge fund risk exposures;
- evaluate the impact of an allocation to a hedge fund strategy in a traditional investment portfolio.

SUMMARY OVERVIEW

- Hedge funds are an important subset of the alternative investments space. Key characteristics distinguishing hedge funds and their strategies from traditional investments include the following: 1) lower legal and regulatory constraints; 2) flexible mandates permitting use of shorting and derivatives; 3) a larger investment universe on which to focus; 4) aggressive investment styles that allow concentrated positions in securities offering exposure to credit, volatility, and liquidity risk premiums; 5) relatively liberal use of leverage; 6) liquidity constraints that include lock-ups and liquidity gates; and 7) relatively high fee structures involving management and incentive fees.

- Hedge fund strategies are classified by a combination of the instruments in which they are invested, the trading philosophy followed, and the types of risks assumed. Some leading hedge fund strategy index providers are Hedge Fund Research; Lipper TASS; Morningstar Hedge/CISDM; Eurekahedge; and Credit Suisse. There is much heterogeneity in the classification and indexes they provide, so no one index group is all-encompassing.

- This chapter classifies hedge fund strategies by the following categories: equity-related strategies; event-driven strategies; relative value strategies; opportunistic strategies; specialist strategies; and multi-manager strategies.

- Equity L/S strategies take advantage of diverse opportunities globally to create alpha via managers' skillful stock picking. Diverse investment styles include value/growth, large cap/small cap, discretionary/quantitative, and industry specialization. Some equity L/S strategies may use index-based short hedges to reduce market risk, but most involve single name shorts for portfolio alpha and added absolute return.

- Equity L/S strategies are typically liquid and generally net long, with gross exposures at 70%–90% long vs. 20%–50% short (but they can vary).

- Equity L/S return profiles are typically aimed to achieve average annual returns roughly equivalent to a long-only approach but with standard deviations that are 50% lower. The more market-neutral or quantitative the strategy approach, the more levered the strategy application to achieve a meaningful return profile.

- Dedicated short sellers only trade with short-side exposure, but they may moderate short beta by also holding cash. Short-biased managers are focused on short-side stock picking, but they typically moderate short beta with some value-oriented long exposure and cash.

- Dedicated short strategies tend to be 60%–120% short at all times, while short-biased strategies are typically around 30%–60% net short. The focus in both cases is usually on single equity stock picking, as opposed to index shorting, and using little if any leverage.

- Dedicated short-selling and short-biased strategies have return goals that are typically less than most other hedge fund strategies but with a negative correlation benefit. Returns are more volatile than a typical L/S equity hedge fund given short beta exposure.

- Equity market-neutral (EMN) strategies take advantage of idiosyncratic short-term mispricing between securities. Their sources of return and alpha do not require accepting beta risk, so EMN strategies are especially attractive in periods of market vulnerability/weakness. There are many types of EMN managers, but most are purely quantitative managers (vs. discretionary managers).

- As many beta risks (e.g., market, sector) are hedged away, EMN strategies generally apply relatively high levels of leverage in striving for meaningful return targets.

- Equity market-neutral strategies exhibit relatively modest return profiles. Portfolios are aimed at market neutrality and with differing constraints to other factor/sector exposures. Generally high levels of diversification and liquidity with lower standard deviation of returns are typical due to an orientation toward mean reversion.

- Merger arbitrage is a relatively liquid strategy. Defined gains come from idiosyncratic, single security takeover situations, but occasional downside shocks can occur when merger deals unexpectedly fail.

- Cross-border M&A usually involves two sets of governmental approvals. M&A deals involving vertical integration often face antitrust scrutiny and thus carry higher risks and offer wider merger spread returns.
- Merger arbitrage strategies have return profiles that are insurance-like, plus a short put option, with relatively high Sharpe ratios; however, left-tail risk is associated with otherwise steady returns. Merger arbitrage managers typically apply moderate to high leverage to generate meaningful target return levels.
- Distressed securities strategies focus on firms in bankruptcy, facing potential bankruptcy, or under financial stress. Hedge fund managers seek inefficiently priced securities before, during, or after the bankruptcy process, which results in either liquidation or reorganization.
- In liquidation, the firm's assets are sold off and securities holders are paid sequentially based on priority of their claims—from senior secured debt, junior secured debt, unsecured debt, convertible debt, preferred stock, and finally common stock.
- In re-organization, a firm's capital structure is re-organized and terms for current claims are negotiated and revised. Debtholders either may agree to maturity extensions or to exchanging their debt for new equity shares (existing shares are canceled) that are sold to new investors to improve the firm's financial condition.
- Outright shorts or hedged positions are possible, but distressed securities investing is usually long-biased, entails relatively high levels of illiquidity, and has moderate to low leverage. The return profile is typically at the higher end of event-driven strategies, but it is more discrete and cyclical.
- For fixed-income arbitrage, the attractiveness of returns is a function of the correlations between different securities, the yield spread pick-up available, and the high number and wide diversity of debt securities across different markets, each having different credit quality and convexity aspects in their pricing.
- Yield curve and carry trades within the US government space are very liquid but have the fewest mispricing opportunities. Liquidity for relative value positions generally decreases in other sovereign markets, mortgage-related markets, and across corporate debt markets.
- Fixed-income arbitrage involves high leverage usage, but leverage availability diminishes with trade and underlying instrument complexity.
- Convertible arbitrage strategies strive to extract "underpriced" implied volatility from long convertible bond holdings. To do this, managers will delta hedge and gamma trade short equity positions against their convertible positions. Convertible arbitrage works best in periods of high convertible issuance, moderate volatility, and reasonable market liquidity.
- Liquidity issues may arise from convertible bonds being naturally less-liquid securities due to their relatively small issue sizes and inherent complexities as well as the availability and cost to borrow underlying equity for short selling.
- Convertible arbitrage managers typically run convertible portfolios at 300% long vs. 200% short. The lower short exposure is a function of the delta-adjusted exposure needed from short sales to balance the long convertibles.
- Global macro strategies focus on correctly discerning and capitalizing on trends in global financial markets using a wide range of instruments. Managed futures strategies have a similar aim but focus on investments using mainly futures and options on futures, on stock and fixed-income indexes, as well as on commodities and currencies.
- Managed futures strategies typically are implemented via more systematic approaches, while global macro strategies tend to use more discretionary approaches. Both strategies are highly liquid and use high leverage.

- Returns of managed futures strategies typically exhibit positive right-tail skewness during market stress. Global macro strategies generally deliver similar diversification in stress periods but with more heterogeneous outcomes.
- Specialist hedge fund strategies require highly specialized skill sets for trading in niche markets. Two such typical specialist strategies—which are aimed at generating uncorrelated, attractive risk-adjusted returns—are volatility trading and reinsurance/life settlements.
- Volatility traders strive to capture relative timing and strike pricing opportunities due to changes in the term structure of volatility. They try to capture volatility smile and skew by using various types of option spreads, such as bull and bear spreads, straddles, and calendar spreads. In addition to using exchange-listed and OTC options, VIX futures, volatility swaps, and variance swaps can be used to implement volatility trading strategies.
- Life settlements strategies involve analyzing pools of life insurance contracts offered by third-party brokers, where the hedge fund purchases the pool and effectively becomes the beneficiary. The hedge fund manager looks for policies with the following traits: 1) The surrender value being offered to the insured individual is relatively low; 2) the ongoing premium payments are also relatively low; and 3) the probability is relatively high that the insured person will die sooner than predicted by standard actuarial methods.
- Funds-of-funds and multi-strategy funds typically offer steady, low-volatility returns via their strategy diversification. Multi-strategy funds have generally outperformed FoFs, but they have more variance due to using relatively high leverage.
- Multi-strategy funds offer potentially faster tactical asset allocation and generally improved fee structure (netting risk between strategies is often at least partially absorbed by the general partner), but they have higher manager-specific operational risks. FoFs offer a potentially more diverse strategy mix, but they have less transparency, slower tactical reaction time, and contribute netting risk to the FoF investor.
- Conditional linear factor models can be useful for uncovering and analyzing hedge fund strategy risk exposures. This chapter uses such a model that incorporates four factors for assessing risk exposures in both normal periods and market stress/crisis periods: equity risk, credit risk, currency risk, and volatility risk.
- Adding a 20% allocation of a hedge fund strategy group to a traditional 60%/40% portfolio (for a 48% stocks/32% bonds/20% hedge funds portfolio) typically decreases total portfolio standard deviation while it increases Sharpe and Sortino ratios (and also often decreases maximum drawdown) in the combined portfolios. This demonstrates that hedge funds act as both risk-adjusted return enhancers and diversifiers for the traditional stock/bond portfolio.

PROBLEMS

1. Bern Zang is the chief investment officer of the Janson University Endowment Investment Office. The Janson University Endowment Fund (the "Fund") is based in the United States and has current assets under management of $10 billion, with minimal exposure to alternative investments. Zang currently seeks to increase the Fund's allocation to hedge funds and considers four strategies: dedicated short bias, merger arbitrage, convertible bond arbitrage, and global macro.

At a meeting with the Fund's board of directors, the board mandates Zang to invest only in event-driven and relative value hedge fund strategies.

Determine, among the four strategies under consideration by Zang, the two that are permitted given the board's mandate. **Justify** your response.

i.   Dedicated short bias
ii. Merger arbitrage
iii. Convertible bond arbitrage
iv. Global macro

Determine, among the four strategies under consideration by Zang, the two that are permitted given the board's mandate. (circle two)	**Justify** your response.
Dedicated short bias	
Merger arbitrage	
Convertible bond arbitrage	
Global macro strategies	

The following information relates to Questions 2 and 3.

Jane Shaindy is the chief investment officer of a large pension fund. The pension fund is based in the United States and currently has minimal exposure to hedge funds. The pension fund's board has recently approved an additional investment in a long/short equity strategy. As part of Shaindy's due diligence on a hedge fund that implements a long/short equity strategy, she uses a conditional linear factor model to uncover and analyze the hedge fund's risk exposures. She is interested in analyzing several risk factors, but she is specifically concerned about whether the hedge fund's long (positive) exposure to equities increases during turbulent market periods.

2. **Describe** how the conditional linear factor model can be used to address Shaindy's concern.

    During a monthly board meeting, Shaindy discusses her updated market forecast for equity markets. Due to a recent large increase in interest rates and geopolitical tensions, her forecast has changed from one of modestly rising equities to several periods of non-trending markets. Given this new market view, Shaindy concludes that a long/short strategy will not be optimal at this time and seeks another equity-related strategy. The Fund has the capacity to use a substantial amount of leverage.

3. **Determine** the *most appropriate* equity-related hedge fund strategy that Shaindy should employ. **Justify** your response.

4. Gunnar Patel is an event-driven hedge fund manager for Senson Fund, which focuses on merger arbitrage strategies. Patel has been monitoring the potential acquisition of Meura Inc. by Sellshom, Inc. Sellshom is currently trading at $60 per share and has offered to buy Meura in a stock-for-stock deal. Meura was trading at $18 per share just prior to the announcement of the acquisition.

   The offer ratio is 1 share of Sellshom in exchange for 2 shares of Meura. Soon after the announcement, Meura's share price jumps to $22 while Sellshom's falls to $55 in anticipation of the merger receiving required approvals and the deal closing successfully.

   At the current share prices of $55 for Sellshom and $22 for Meura, Patel attempts to profit from the merger announcement. He buys 40,000 shares of Meura and sells short 20,000 shares of Sellshom.

   Calculate the payoffs of the merger arbitrage under the following two scenarios:
   i. The merger is successfully completed.
   ii. The merger fails.

5. John Puten is the chief investment officer of the Markus University Endowment Investment Office. Puten seeks to increase the diversification of the endowment by investing in hedge funds. He recently met with several hedge fund managers that employ different investment strategies. In selecting a hedge fund manager, Puten prefers to hire a manager that uses the following:
   • Fundamental and technical analysis to value markets
   • Discretionary and systematic modes of implementation
   • Top-down strategies
   • A range of macroeconomic and fundamental models to express a view regarding the direction or relative value of a particular asset

   Puten's staff prepares a brief summary of two potential hedge fund investments:

   Hedge Fund 1: A relative value strategy fund focusing only on convertible arbitrage.
   Hedge Fund 2: An opportunistic strategy fund focusing only on global macro strategies.

   Determine which hedge fund would be *most appropriate* for Puten.
   Justify your response.

6. Yankel Stein is the chief investment officer of a large charitable foundation based in the United States. Although the foundation has significant exposure to alternative investments and hedge funds, Stein proposes to increase the foundation's exposure to relative value hedge fund strategies. As part of Stein's due diligence on a hedge fund engaging in convertible bond arbitrage, Stein asks his investment analyst to summarize different risks associated with the strategy.

   Describe how each of the following circumstances can create concerns for Stein's proposed hedge fund strategy:
   i.   Short selling
   ii. Credit issues
   iii. Time decay of call option
   iv. Extreme market volatility

	Describe how each of the following circumstances can create concerns for Stein's proposed hedge fund strategy:
Short selling	
Credit issues	
Time decay of call option	
Extreme market volatility	

The following information relates to Questions 7 and 8.

Sushil Wallace is the chief investment officer of a large pension fund. Wallace wants to increase the pension fund's allocation to hedge funds and recently met with three hedge fund managers. These hedge funds focus on the following strategies:

Hedge Fund A: Specialist—Follows relative value volatility arbitrage
Hedge Fund B: Multi-manager—Multi-strategy fund
Hedge Fund C: Multi-manager—Fund-of-funds

7. **Describe** three paths for implementing the strategy of Hedge Fund A.

   After a significant amount of internal discussion, Wallace concludes that the pension fund should invest in either Hedge Fund B or C for the diversification benefits from the different strategies employed. However, after final due diligence is completed, Wallace recommends investing only in Hedge Fund B, noting its many advantages over Hedge Fund C.

8. **Discuss** *two* advantages of Hedge Fund B relative to Hedge Fund C with respect to investment characteristics.

9. Kloss Investments is an investment adviser whose clients are small institutional investors. Muskogh Charitable Foundation (the "Foundation") is a client with $70 million of assets under management. The Foundation has a traditional asset allocation of 65% stocks/35% bonds. Risk and return characteristics for the Foundation's current portfolio are presented in Panel A of Exhibit 1.

   Kloss' CIO, Christine Singh, recommends to Muskogh's investment committee that it should add a 10% allocation to hedge funds. The investment committee indicates to Singh that Muskogh's primary considerations for the Foundation's portfolio are that any hedge fund strategy allocation should: a) limit volatility, b) maximize risk-adjusted returns, and c) limit downside risk.

   Singh's associate prepares expected risk and return characteristics for three portfolios that have allocations of 60% stocks, 30% bonds, and 10% hedge funds, where the 10% hedge fund allocation follows either an equity market-neutral, global macro, or convertible arbitrage strategy. The risk and return characteristics of the three portfolios are presented in Panel B of Exhibit 1.

EXHIBIT 1

Hedge Fund Strategy	SD (%)	Sharpe Ratio	Sortino Ratio	Maximum Drawdown (%)
Panel A: Current Portfolio				
N/A	8.75	0.82	1.25	16.2
Panel B: Three Potential Portfolios with a 10% Hedge Fund Allocation				
Equity market neutral	8.72	0.80	1.21	15.1
Global macro	8.55	0.95	1.35	15.0
Convertible arbitrage	8.98	0.83	1.27	20.2

Discuss which hedge fund strategy Singh should view as most suitable for meeting the considerations expressed by Muskogh's investment committee.

The following information relates to Questions 10–17.

Snohomish Mukilteo is a portfolio analyst for the Puyallup-Wenatchee Pension Fund (PWPF). PWPF's investment committee (IC) asks Mukilteo to research adding hedge funds to the PWPF portfolio.

A member of the IC meets with Mukilteo to discuss hedge fund strategies. During the meeting, the IC member admits that her knowledge of hedge fund strategies is fairly limited but tells Mukilteo she believes the following:

Statement 1:   Equity market-neutral strategies use a relative value approach.
Statement 2:   Event-driven strategies are not exposed to equity market beta risk.
Statement 3:   Opportunistic strategies have risk exposure to market directionality.

The IC member also informs Mukilteo that for equity-related strategies, the IC considers low volatility to be more important than negative correlation.

Mukilteo researches various hedge fund strategies. First, Mukilteo analyzes an event-driven strategy involving two companies, Algona Applications (AA) and Tukwila Technologies (TT). AA's management, believing that its own shares are overvalued, uses its shares to acquire TT. The IC has expressed concern about this type of strategy because of the potential for loss if the acquisition unexpectedly fails. Mukilteo's research reveals a way to use derivatives to protect against this loss, and he believes that such protection will satisfy the IC's concern.

Next, while researching relative value strategies, Mukilteo considers a government bond strategy that involves buying lower-liquidity, off-the-run bonds and selling higher-liquidity, duration-matched, on-the-run bonds.

Mukilteo examines an opportunistic strategy implemented by one of the hedge funds under consideration. The hedge fund manager selects 12 AAA rated corporate bonds with actively traded futures contracts and approximately equal durations. For each corporate bond, the manager calculates the 30-day change in the yield spread over a constant risk-free rate. He then ranks the bonds according to this spread change. For the bonds that show the greatest spread narrowing (widening), the hedge fund will take long (short) positions in their futures contracts. The net holding for this strategy is market neutral.

Mukilteo also plans to recommend a specialist hedge fund strategy that would allow PWPF to maintain a high Sharpe ratio even during a financial crisis when equity markets fall.

The IC has been considering the benefits of allocating to a fund of funds (FoF) or to a multi-strategy fund (MSF). Mukilteo receives the following email from a member of the IC:

> *From my perspective, an FoF is superior even though it entails higher manager-specific operational risk and will require us to pay a double layer of fees without being able to net performance fees on individual managers. I especially like the tactical allocation advantage of FoFs—that they are more likely to be well informed about when to tactically reallocate to a particular strategy and more capable of shifting capital between strategies quickly.*

Finally, Mukilteo creates a model to simulate adding selected individual hedge fund strategies to the current portfolio with a 20% allocation. The IC's primary considerations for a combined portfolio are: (1) that the variance of the combined portfolio must be less than 90% of that of the current portfolio and (2) that the combined portfolio maximize the risk-adjusted return with the expectation of large negative events. Exhibit 2 provides historical performance and risk metrics for three simulated portfolios.

EXHIBIT 2   Performance of Various Combined Portfolios

Hedge Fund Strategy	Standard Deviation(%)	Sharpe Ratio	Sortino Ratio	Maximum Drawdown (%)
Current Portfolio				
NA	7.95	0.58	1.24	14.18
Three Potential Portfolios with a 20% Hedge Fund Allocation				
Merger arbitrage	7.22	0.73	1.35	5.60
Systematic futures	6.94	0.83	1.68	8.04
Equity market neutral	7.17	0.73	1.80	10.72

10. Which of the IC member's statements regarding hedge fund strategies is *incorrect*?
    A. Statement 1
    B. Statement 2
    C. Statement 3
11. Based on what the IC considers important for equity-related strategies, which strategy should Mukilteo *most likely* avoid?
    A. Long/short equity
    B. Equity market neutral
    C. Dedicated short selling and short biased

12. Which of the following set of derivative positions will *most likely* satisfy the IC's concern about the event-driven strategy involving AA and TT?
    A. Long out-of-the-money puts on AA shares and long out-of-the-money calls on TT shares
    B. Long out-of-the-money calls on AA shares and long out-of-the-money puts on TT shares
    C. Long risk-free bonds, short out-of-the-money puts on AA shares, and long out-of-the-money calls on TT shares
13. The government bond strategy that Mukilteo considers is *best* described as a:
    A. carry trade.
    B. yield curve trade.
    C. long/short credit trade.
14. The opportunistic strategy that Mukilteo considers is *most likely* to be described as a:
    A. global macro strategy.
    B. time-series momentum strategy.
    C. cross-sectional momentum strategy.
15. The specialist hedge fund strategy that Mukilteo plans to recommend is *most likely*:
    A. cross-asset volatility trading between the US and Japanese markets.
    B. selling equity volatility and collecting the volatility risk premium.
    C. buying longer-dated out-of-the-money options on VIX index futures.
16. Based on the email that Mukilteo received, the IC member's perspective is correct with regard to:
    A. layering and netting of fees.
    B. tactical allocation capabilities.
    C. manager-specific operational risks.
17. Based on the IC's primary considerations for a combined portfolio, which simulated hedge fund strategy portfolio in Exhibit 1 creates the *most suitable* combined portfolio?
    A. Merger arbitrage
    B. Systematic futures
    C. Equity market neutral

The following information relates to Questions 18–23.

Lynet Xu is the chief investment officer for the North University Endowment Fund (the Fund), which is based in Europe. The Fund's investment committee recently made the decision to add hedge funds to the Fund's portfolio to increase diversification. Xu meets with Yolanda Anderson, a junior analyst, to discuss various hedge fund strategies that might be suitable for the Fund. Anderson tells Xu the following:

Statement 1: Relative value strategies tend to use minimal leverage.

Statement 2: Long/short equity strategies are typically not exposed to equity market beta risk.

Statement 3: Global macro strategies come with naturally higher volatility in the return profiles typically delivered.

Xu tells Anderson that while she is open to using all hedge fund strategies, she is particularly interested in opportunistic hedge fund strategies. Xu states that she prefers opportunistic hedge fund strategies that use high leverage, have high liquidity, and exhibit right-tail skewness.

Xu asks Anderson to research an event-driven strategy involving a potential merger between Aqua Company and Taurus, Inc. Aqua has offered to buy Taurus in a stock-for-stock deal: The offer ratio is two shares of Aqua for three shares of Taurus. Aqua was trading at €50 per share prior to the merger announcement, and it fell to €45 per share after the merger announcement. Taurus was trading at €15 per share prior to the announcement, and it rose to €20 per share in anticipation of the merger deal receiving required approvals and closing successfully. Xu decides to enter into a merger arbitrage trade: She buys 22,500 shares of Taurus at €20 per share and sells short 15,000 shares of Aqua at €45 per share.

Xu and Anderson discuss an equity strategy involving two large European car companies, ZMD and Tarreras. Anderson recently attended a trade show where she inspected ZMD's newest model car. Based on information from the trade show and other analysis conducted by Anderson, Xu concludes that ZMD will not meet its revenue expectations. Current valuation metrics indicate that ZMD shares are overvalued relative to shares of Tarreras. Xu decides to take a short position in ZMD and a long position in Tarreras with equal beta-weighted exposure.

Xu next reviews a convertible arbitrage strategy and analyzes a trade involving the euro-denominated stock and convertible bonds of AVC Corporation, a European utility company. Anderson gathers selected data for AVC Corporation, which is presented in Exhibit 3.

EXHIBIT 3   Selected Data for AVC Corporation

AVC Convertible Bond		AVC Stock	
Price (% of par)	115	Current price (per share)	€28
Coupon (%)	6	P/E	25
Remaining maturity (years)	2	P/BV	2.25
Conversion ratio	50	P/CF	15

Based on comparisons with industry ratios, Xu believes that AVC's shares are overvalued in relative terms and the convertible bonds are undervalued. Anderson analyzes the potential profit outcomes of a long position in the convertible bond combined with a short stock position, assuming small changes in the share price and ignoring dividends and borrowing costs. She offers the following conclusion to Xu: "The profit earned on the convertible arbitrage trade will be the same regardless of whether the share price of AVC decreases or increases."

Finally, Xu and Anderson consider a hedge fund that specializes in reinsurance and life settlements. Xu tells Anderson about three characteristics that hedge fund managers look for when investing in life settlements:

Characteristic 1:   The surrender value offered to the insured individual is relatively high.

Characteristic 2:   The ongoing premium payments to keep the policy active are relatively low.

Characteristic 3:   There is a high probability that the designated insured person is likely to die within the period predicted by standard actuarial methods.

18. Which of Anderson's three statements regarding hedge fund strategies is correct?
    A. Statement 1
    B. Statement 2
    C. Statement 3
19. Which opportunistic hedge fund strategy meets Xu's preferences?
    A. Only global macro
    B. Only managed futures
    C. Both global macro and managed futures
20. Assuming the merger between Aqua and Taurus successfully closes, the payoff on Xu's merger arbitrage trade will be:
    A. −€187,500.
    B. €225,000.
    C. €412,500.
21. Which equity hedge fund strategy *best* describes the ZMD and Tarreras positions taken by Xu?
    A. Short bias
    B. Long/short equity
    C. Equity market neutral
22. Anderson's conclusion about the profitability of the AVC convertible arbitrage trade is:
    A. correct.
    B. incorrect, because the profit will be higher if the share price decreases.
    C. incorrect, because the profit will be higher if the share price increases.
23. Which of the three characteristics of life settlements noted by Anderson is correct?
    A. Characteristic 1
    B. Characteristic 2
    C. Characteristic 3

HEDGE FUND STRATEGIES

SOLUTIONS

1.

Determine, among the four strategies under consideration by Zang, the two that are permitted given the board's mandate. (circle two)	**Justify** your response.
Dedicated short bias	A dedicated short bias hedge fund strategy is an example of an equity hedge fund strategy, not an event-driven or relative value strategy. Equity hedge fund strategies focus primarily on the equity markets, and the majority of their risk profiles contain equity-oriented risk. Dedicated short bias managers look for possible short selling targets among companies that are overvalued, that are experiencing declining revenues and/or earnings, or that have internal management conflicts, weak corporate governance, or even potential accounting frauds.
Merger arbitrage	A merger arbitrage hedge fund strategy is an example of an event-driven strategy, which is permitted under the board's mandate. Event-driven hedge fund strategies focus on corporate events, such as governance events, mergers and acquisitions, bankruptcy, and other key events for corporations. Merger arbitrage involves simultaneously purchasing and selling the stocks of two merging companies to create "riskless" profits.

Convertible bond arbitrage	A convertible bond arbitrage hedge fund strategy is an example of a relative value strategy, which is permitted under the board's mandate. Relative value hedge fund strategies focus on the relative valuation between two or more securities. Relative value strategies are often exposed to credit and liquidity risks because the valuation differences from which these strategies seek to benefit are often due to differences in credit quality and/or liquidity across different securities. A classic convertible bond arbitrage strategy is to buy the relatively undervalued convertible bond and take a short position in the relatively overvalued underlying stock.
Global macro	A global macro hedge fund strategy is an example of an opportunistic hedge fund strategy, not an event-driven or relative value strategy. Opportunistic hedge fund strategies take a top-down approach, focus on a multi-asset opportunity set, and include global macro strategies. Global macro managers use both fundamental and technical analysis to value markets as well as discretionary and systematic modes of implementation.

2. A linear factor model can provide insights into the intrinsic characteristics and risks in a hedge fund investment. Since hedge fund strategies are dynamic, a conditional model allows for the analysis in a specific market environment to determine whether hedge fund strategies are exposed to certain risks under abnormal market conditions. A conditional model can show whether hedge fund risk exposures to equities that are insignificant during calm periods become significant during turbulent market periods. During normal periods when equities are rising, the desired exposure to equities (S&P 500 Index) should be long (positive) to benefit from higher expected returns. However, during crisis periods when equities are falling sharply, the desired exposure to equities should be short (negative).

3. Shaindy should employ an equity market-neutral (EMN) equity strategy. Overall, EMN managers are more useful for portfolio allocation during periods of non-trending or declining markets. EMN hedge fund strategies take opposite (long and short) positions in similar or related equities having divergent valuations while attempting to maintain a near net zero portfolio exposure to the market. EMN managers neutralize market risk by constructing their portfolios such that the expected portfolio beta is approximately equal to zero. Moreover, EMN managers often choose to set the betas for sectors or industries as well as for common risk factors (e.g., market size, price-to-earnings ratio, and book-to-market ratio) equal to zero. Since these portfolios do not take beta risk and attempt to neutralize many other factor risks, they typically must apply leverage to the long and short positions to achieve a meaningful return profile from their individual stock selections.

   EMN strategies typically deliver return profiles that are steadier and less volatile than those of many other hedge strategy areas. Over time, their conservative and constrained approach typically results in a less dynamic overall return profile than those of managers who accept beta exposure. Despite the use of substantial leverage and because of their more standard and overall steady risk/return profiles, equity market-neutral managers are often a preferred replacement for fixed-income managers during periods when fixed-income returns are unattractively low.

4.

   i. At the current share prices of $55 for Sellshom and $22 for Meura, Patel would receive $1,100,000 from short selling 20,000 shares of Sellshom and would pay $880,000 to buy 40,000 shares of Meura. This provides a net spread of $220,000 to Patel if the merger is successfully completed.

  ii. If the merger fails, then prices should revert back to their pre-merger announcement levels of $18 per share for Meura and $60 per share for Sellshom. The manager would need to buy back 20,000 shares of Sellshom at $60 per share, for a total of $1,200,000, to close the short position. Patel would then sell the long position of 40,000 shares of Meura at $18 per share for a total of $720,000. This net loss would be $260,000, calculated as: (Sellshom: $1,100,000 – $1,200,000 = –$100,000) + (Meura: –$880,000 + $720,000 = –$160,000).

5. Hedge Fund 2 would be most appropriate for Puten because it follows a global macro strategy, which is consistent with Puten's preferences. Global macro managers use both fundamental and technical analysis to value markets, and they use discretionary and systematic modes of implementation. The key source of returns in global macro strategies revolves around correctly discerning and capitalizing on trends in global markets.

     Global macro strategies are typically top-down and employ a range of macroeconomic and fundamental models to express a view regarding the direction or relative value of a particular asset or asset class. Positions may comprise a mix of individual securities, baskets of securities, index futures, foreign exchange futures/forwards, fixed-income products or futures, and derivatives or options on any of the above. If the hedge fund manager is making a directional bet, then directional models will use fundamental data regarding a specific market or asset to determine if it is undervalued or overvalued relative to history and the expected macro-trend.

     Hedge Fund 1 follows a relative value strategy with a focus on convertible arbitrage, which is not aligned with Puten's preferences. In a convertible bond arbitrage strategy, the manager strives to extract "cheap" implied volatility by buying the relatively undervalued convertible bond and taking a short position in the relatively overvalued common stock. Convertible arbitrage managers are typically neither using fundamental and technical analysis to value markets nor employing top-down strategies to express a view regarding the direction or relative value of an asset.

6.

	Describe how each of the following circumstances can create concerns for Stein's proposed hedge fund strategy:
Short selling	Since Hedge Fund 1 employs a convertible arbitrage strategy, the fund buys the convertible bond and takes a short position in the underlying security. When short selling, shares must be located and borrowed; as a result, the stock owner may want his/her shares returned at a potentially inopportune time, such as during stock price run-ups or when supply for the stock is low or demand for the stock is high. This situation, particularly a short squeeze, can lead to substantial losses and a suddenly unbalanced exposure if borrowing the underlying equity shares becomes too difficult or too costly for the arbitrageur.
Credit issues	Credit issues may complicate valuation since bonds have exposure to credit risk. When credit spreads widen or narrow, there would be a mismatch in the values of the stock and convertible bond positions that the convertible manager may or may not have attempted to hedge away.

Time decay of call option	The convertible bond arbitrage strategy can lose money due to time decay of the convertible bond's embedded call option during periods of reduced realized equity volatility and/or due to a general compression of market implied volatility levels.
Extreme market volatility	Convertible arbitrage strategies have performed best when convertible issuance is high (implying a wider choice among convertible securities as well as downward price pressure and cheaper prices), general market volatility levels are moderate, and the liquidity to trade and adjust positions is sufficient. Extreme market volatility typically implies heightened credit risks. Convertibles are naturally less-liquid securities, so convertible managers generally do not fare well during such periods. Because hedge funds have become the natural market makers for convertibles and typically face significant redemption pressures from investors during crises, the strategy may have further unattractive left-tail risk attributes during periods of market stress.

7. Hedge Fund A's volatility trading strategy can be implemented by following multiple paths. One path is through simple exchange-traded options. The maturity of such options typically extends to no more than two years. In terms of expiry, the longer-dated options will have more absolute exposure to volatility levels than shorter-dated options, but the shorter-dated options will exhibit more delta sensitivity to price changes.

A second, similar path is to implement the volatility trading strategy using OTC options. In this case, the tenor and strike prices of the options can be customized. The tenor of expiry dates can then be extended beyond what is available with exchange-traded options.

A third path is to use VIX futures or options on VIX futures as a way to more explicitly express a pure volatility view without the need for constant delta hedging of an equity put or call for isolating the volatility exposure.

A fourth path for implementing a volatility trading strategy would be to purchase an OTC volatility swap or a variance swap from a creditworthy counterparty. A volatility swap is a forward contract on future realized price volatility. Similarly, a variance swap is a forward contract on future realized price variance, where variance is the square of volatility. Both volatility and variance swaps provide "pure" exposure to volatility alone, unlike standardized options in which the volatility exposure depends on the price of the underlying asset and must be isolated and extracted via delta hedging.

8.

A. Multi-strategy managers like Hedge Fund B can reallocate capital into different strategy areas more quickly and efficiently than would be possible by a fund-of-funds (FoF) manager like Hedge Fund C. The multi-strategy manager has full transparency and a better picture of the interactions of the different teams' portfolio risks than would ever be possible for FoF managers to achieve. Consequently, the multi-strategy manager can react faster to different real-time market impacts—for example, by rapidly increasing or decreasing leverage within different strategies depending upon the perceived riskiness of available opportunities.

B. The fees paid by investors in a multi-strategy fund can be structured in a number of ways, some of which can be very attractive when compared to the FoFs' added fee layering and netting risk attributes. Conceptually, FoF investors always face netting risk, whereby they are responsible for paying performance fees due to winning underlying funds while suffering return drag from the performance of losing underlying funds. Even if the FoF's overall performance is flat or down, FoF investors must still pay incentive fees due to the managers of winning funds.

9. Based on the investment committee's considerations, Singh should view a 10% allocation to the global macro hedge fund strategy as most suitable for the Foundation. Such an allocation would result in a decrease in standard deviation (volatility) and significant increases in the combined portfolio's Sharpe and Sortino ratios (these are the highest such ratios among the strategies presented). In addition, the lower maximum drawdown (15.0%) indicates less downside risk in the combined portfolio than with any of the other strategy choices.

10. B is correct. Statement 2 is incorrect. Event-driven strategies, such as merger arbitrage, tend to be exposed to some natural equity market beta risk. Overall market risk can potentially disrupt a merger's consummation (though hedging may be possible). To the extent that deals are more likely to fail in market stress periods, event-driven merger arbitrage strategies have market sensitivity and left-tail risk attributes. Also, while event-driven strategies may have less beta exposure than simple, long-only beta allocations, the higher hedge fund fees effectively result in a particularly expensive form of embedded beta. Equity market-neutral strategies do use a relative value approach, because such strategies hold balanced long and short equity exposures to maintain zero (or close to zero) net exposure to the equity market and such factors as sector and size. Also, opportunistic strategies do have risk exposure to market directionality, also called trendiness.

    A is incorrect because equity market-neutral strategies do use a relative value approach. Equity market-neutral strategies hold balanced long and short equity exposures to maintain zero (or close to zero) net exposure to the equity market and such factors as sector and size (i.e., market cap). They then focus on, for example, pairs of long and short securities whose prices are out of historical alignment and are expected to experience mean reversion. To take advantage of idiosyncratic short-term mispricing between securities whose prices should otherwise be co-integrated, equity market-neutral hedge fund strategies take opposite (i.e., long and short) positions in similar or related equities that have divergent valuations, while also attempting to maintain a near net zero portfolio exposure to the market.

    C is incorrect because opportunistic strategies do have risk exposure to market directionality, also called trendiness. Opportunistic strategies are based on macro themes and multi-asset relationships on a global basis; therefore, broad themes, global relationships, market trends, and cycles affect their returns. Generally, the key source of returns in global macro strategies revolves around correctly discerning and capitalizing on trends in global markets. For example, global macro managers typically hold views on trends in inflation (among other things). Global macro strategies are typically top down and use a range of macroeconomic and fundamental models to express a view regarding the direction or relative value of an asset or asset class. If the hedge fund manager is making a directional bet, then directional models will use fundamental data regarding a specific market or asset to determine whether it is undervalued or overvalued relative to history and the expected macro trend.

11. C is correct. For equity-related strategies, the IC considers low volatility to be more important than negative correlation. Dedicated short selling and short-biased strategies have return goals that are typically less than those for most other hedge fund strategies but with a negative correlation benefit. In addition, they are more volatile than a typical long/short equity hedge fund because of their short beta exposure. As a result, Mukilteo should avoid dedicated short selling and short-biased strategies.

A is incorrect because long/short equity is a lower-volatility strategy. A long/short equity manager aims to achieve a standard deviation that is 50% lower than a long-only approach while achieving average annual returns roughly equivalent to a long-only approach. Since the IC considers low volatility important, this is not a strategy that Mukilteo should necessarily avoid.

B is incorrect because equity market-neutral strategies generally have high levels of diversification and lower standard deviations of returns than many other strategies across normal market conditions. Because they typically deliver returns that are steadier and less volatile than those of many other hedge strategy areas, equity market-neutral managers generally are more useful for portfolio allocation during periods of non-trending or declining markets. Equity market-neutral managers neutralize market risk by constructing their portfolios such that the expected portfolio beta is approximately equal to zero. Over time, their conservative and constrained approach typically results in less volatile overall returns than those of managers who accept beta exposure. (The exception to this norm is when the use of significant leverage may cause forced portfolio downsizing.) Since the IC considers low volatility important, this is not a strategy that Mukilteo should necessarily avoid.

12. B is correct. The event-driven strategy that Mukilteo researches is a stock-for-stock merger arbitrage strategy. In this strategy, because the management of the acquiring company (AA) believes its shares to be overvalued, it will offer AA shares in exchange for target company (TT) shares in a specified ratio. The merger arbitrage fund manager will then buy TT shares and sell AA shares in the same ratio as the offer, hoping to earn the spread on successful deal completion.

For most acquisitions, the initial announcement of a deal will cause the target's share price to rise toward the acquisition price and the acquirer's share price to fall (either because of the potential dilution of its outstanding shares or the use of cash for purposes other than a dividend payment). If the acquisition is unsuccessful, the manager faces losses if the target's share price has already risen and/or the acquirer's share price has already fallen in anticipation of the acquisition. When merger deals do fail, the initial price rise of the target's shares and the initial price fall of the acquirer's shares are typically reversed. Arbitrageurs who jumped into the merger situation after its initial announcement stand to incur substantial losses on their long positions in the target's shares and their short positions in the acquirer's shares.

To manage the risk of the acquisition failing, the manager can buy out-of-the-money calls on AA shares (to cover the short position) and buy out-of-the money puts on TT shares (to protect against loss in value). Such a position will provide protection that would likely satisfy the IC's concern about losses with this strategy.

A is incorrect because protecting against loss with this strategy requires buying out-of-the-money calls (not puts) on AA and buying out-of-the-money puts (not calls) on TT.

C is incorrect because it represents the payoff profile of this merger arbitrage strategy, not a way to protect the strategy against loss should the acquisition fail. The payoff profile of this merger arbitrage strategy resembles that of a riskless bond combined with a short put option on AA shares and a long call option on TT shares. The short put on the AA shares reflects the need to cover the short position in AA when the share price rises. The long call on TT shares becomes valuable if and when another interested acquirer (i.e., White Knight) makes a higher bid for TT before the initial merger proposal is completed.

13. A is correct. Carry trades involve going long a higher-yielding security and shorting a lower-yielding security with the expectation of receiving the positive carry and of profiting on

long and short sides of the trade when the temporary relative mispricing reverts to normal. A classic example of a fixed-income arbitrage trade involves buying lower-liquidity, off-the-run government securities and selling higher-liquidity, duration-matched, on-the-run government securities. Interest rate and credit risks are hedged because long and short positions have the same duration and credit exposure. So, the key concern is liquidity risk. Under normal conditions, as time passes, the more (less) expensive on-the-run (off-the-run) securities will decrease (increase) in price as the current on-the-runs are replaced by a more liquid issue of new on-the-run bonds that then become off-the-run bonds.

B is incorrect because Mukilteo considers a carry trade, not a yield curve trade. For yield curve trades, the prevalent calendar spread strategy involves taking long and short positions at different points on the yield curve where the relative mispricing of securities offers the best opportunities, such as in a curve flattening or steepening, to profit. Perceptions and forecasts of macroeconomic conditions are the backdrop for these types of trades. The positions can be in fixed-income securities of the same issuer; in that case, most credit and liquidity risks would likely be hedged, making interest rate risk the main concern. Alternatively, longs and shorts can be taken in the securities of different issuers—but typically ones operating in the same industry or sector. In this case, differences in credit quality, liquidity, volatility, and issue-specific characteristics would likely drive the relative mispricing. In either case, the hedge fund manager aims to profit as the mispricing reverses (mean reversion occurs) and the longs rise and shorts fall in value within the targeted time frame.

C is incorrect because Mukilteo considers a carry trade, not a long/short credit trade. In a long/short credit trade, valuation differences result from differences in credit quality—for example, investment-grade versus non-investment-grade securities. It involves the relative credit risks across different security issuers and tends to be naturally more volatile than the exploitation of small pricing differences within sovereign debt alone.

14. C is correct. The strategy under consideration is a managed futures strategy—specifically, a cross-sectional momentum approach. Such an approach is generally implemented with securities in the same asset class, which is corporate bonds in this case. The strategy is to take long positions in contracts for bonds that have risen the most in value relative to the others (the bonds with the narrowing spreads) and short positions in contracts for bonds that have fallen the most in value relative to the others (the bonds with the widening spreads). Cross-sectional momentum strategies generally result in holding a net zero or market-neutral position. In contrast, positions for assets in time-series momentum strategies are determined in isolation, independent of the performance of the other assets in the strategy and can be net long or net short depending on the current price trend of an asset.

A is incorrect because the opportunistic strategy under consideration is more likely to be described as a managed futures strategy—specifically, a cross-sectional momentum approach—rather than a global macro strategy. Global macro strategies are typically top down and generally focus on correctly discerning and capitalizing on trends in global financial markets, which does not describe the strategy under consideration. In contrast, managed futures strategies that use a cross-sectional momentum approach are implemented with a cross-section of assets (generally within an asset class, which in this case is highly rated corporate bonds) by going long those that are rising in price the most and by shorting those that are falling the most.

B is incorrect because the strategy under consideration is a managed futures strategy—specifically, a cross-sectional (not time-series) momentum approach. Time-series trading strategies are driven by the past performance of the individual assets. The manager will take long positions for assets that are rising in value and short positions for assets that are falling in value. Positions are taken on an absolute basis, and individual positions are determined independent of the performance of the other assets in the strategy. This approach is in contrast to cross-sectional strategies, where the position taken in an asset depends on that asset's performance relative to the other assets. With time-series momentum strategies, the manager can be net long or net short depending on the current price trend of an asset.

15. C is correct. Mukilteo needs to recommend a specialist hedge fund strategy that can help PWPF maintain a high Sharpe ratio even in a crisis when equity markets fall. Buying longer-dated out-of-the-money options on VIX index futures is a long equity volatility position that works as a protective hedge, particularly in an equity market crisis when volatility spikes and equity prices fall. A long volatility strategy is a useful potential diversifier for long equity investments (albeit at the cost of the option premium paid by the volatility buyer). Because equity volatility is approximately 80% negatively correlated with equity market returns, a long position in equity volatility can substantially reduce the portfolio's standard deviation, which would serve to increase its Sharpe ratio. Longer-dated options will have more absolute exposure to volatility levels (i.e., vega exposure) than shorter-dated options, and out-of-the-money options will typically trade at higher implied volatility levels than at-the-money options.

   A is incorrect because cross-asset volatility trading, a type of relative value volatility trading, may often involve idiosyncratic, macro-oriented risks that may have adverse effects during an equity market crisis.

   B is incorrect because the volatility seller is the provider of insurance during crises, not the beneficiary of it. Selling volatility provides a volatility risk premium or compensation for taking on the risk of providing insurance against crises for holders of equities and other securities. On the short side, option premium sellers generally extract steadier returns in normal market environments.

16. A is correct. FoFs have double layers of fees without being able to net performance fees on individual managers. The FoF investor always faces netting risk and is responsible for paying performance fees that are due to winning underlying funds while suffering return drag from the performance of losing underlying funds. Even if the FoF's overall performance (aggregated across all funds) is flat or down, FoF investors must still pay incentive fees that are due to the managers of the winning underlying funds.

   The fee structure is more investor friendly at MSFs, where the general partner absorbs the netting risk arising from the divergent performance of the fund's different strategy teams. This is an attractive outcome for the MSF investor because: (1) the GP is responsible for netting risk and (2) the only investor-level incentive fees paid are those due on the total fund performance after netting the positive and negative performances of the various strategy teams.

   However, if the MSF operates with a pass-through fee model, the investor will pay for a portion of the netting risk. Using this model, the MSF may charge no management fee but instead pass through the costs of paying individual teams (inclusive of salary and incentives fees earned by each team) before an added manager-level incentive fee is charged to the investor on total fund performance. In this instance, the investor does implicitly pay for a portion of netting risk.

   B is incorrect because MSFs have a tactical allocation advantage over FoFs. MSFs can reallocate capital into different strategy areas more quickly and efficiently than is possible in FoFs, allowing MSFs to react faster to real-time market impacts. This shorter tactical reaction time, combined with MSFs' better strategy transparency, makes MSFs more resilient than FoFs in preserving capital.

C is incorrect because MSFs have higher manager-specific operational risks than FoFs. In MSFs, teams of managers dedicated to running different hedge fund strategies share operational and risk management systems under the same roof. This means that the MSF's operational risks are not well diversified because all operational processes are performed under the same fund structure. FoFs, in contrast, have less operational risk because each separate underlying hedge fund is responsible for its own risk management.

17. C is correct. The equity market-neutral strategy makes for a combined portfolio that has a standard deviation below the maximum specified and has the highest Sortino ratio.

The primary consideration is that the variance of the combined portfolio must be less than 90% of that of the current portfolio. Since variance is the square of standard deviation, the maximum variance allowed is:

$$\sigma^2_{max} = (\sigma_{current})^2 \times 90\%$$
$$\sigma^2_{max} = (7.95)^2 \times 90\% = 63.20 \times 0.9 = 56.88$$

And standard deviation is the square root of variance, so the maximum standard deviation allowed is

$$\sigma_{max} = \sqrt{\sigma^2_{max}}$$
$$\sigma_{max} = \sqrt{56.88} = 7.54$$

All three portfolios are below the maximum specified variance.

The next consideration is that the portfolio should maximize the risk-adjusted return with the expectation of large negative events. For hedge fund strategies with large negative events, the Sortino ratio is a more appropriate measure of risk-adjusted return than the Sharpe ratio. The Sharpe ratio measures risk-adjusted performance, where risk is defined as standard deviation, so it penalizes both upside and downside variability. The Sortino ratio measures risk-adjusted performance, where risk is defined as downside deviation, so it penalizes only downside variability below a minimum target return. Of the portfolios that meet the variance requirement, the one with the highest Sortino ratio is the portfolio with the equity market-neutral allocation, with a Sortino ratio of 1.80. Therefore, the portfolio with the equity market-neutral allocation is the most suitable portfolio for the considerations specified by the IC.

A is incorrect because the portfolio with an allocation to the merger arbitrage hedge fund strategy, while meeting the variance requirement, has a lower Sortino ratio (1.35) than the portfolio with an allocation to the equity market-neutral hedge fund strategy (1.80). Although the portfolio with the merger arbitrage allocation has the lowest value of maximum drawdown (5.60), the relevant measure of downside risk is the Sortino ratio. As a result, the portfolio with the equity market-neutral allocation is the most suitable portfolio given the considerations specified by the IC.

B is incorrect because the portfolio with an allocation to the systematic futures hedge fund strategy, while meeting the variance requirement, has a lower Sortino ratio (1.68) than the portfolio with an allocation to the equity market-neutral hedge fund strategy. As a result, the portfolio with the equity market-neutral allocation is the most suitable portfolio given the considerations specified by the IC.

18. C is correct. Global macro investing may introduce natural benefits of asset class and investment approach diversification, but they come with naturally higher volatility in the return profiles typically delivered. The exposures selected in any global macro strategy may not react to the global risks as expected because of either unforeseen contrary factors or global risks that simply do not materialize; thus, macro managers tend to produce somewhat lumpier and more uneven return streams than other hedge fund strategies.

   A is incorrect because relative value hedge fund strategies tend to use significant leverage that can be dangerous to limited partner investors, especially during periods of market stress. During normal market conditions, successful relative value strategies can earn credit, liquidity, or volatility premiums over time. However, in crisis periods when excessive leverage, deteriorating credit quality, illiquidity, and volatility spikes come to fruition, relative value strategies can result in losses.

   B is incorrect because long/short equity strategies tend to be exposed to some natural equity market beta risk but have less beta exposure than simple long-only beta allocations. Given that equity markets tend to rise over the long run, most long/short equity managers typically hold net long equity positions with some managers maintaining their short positions as a hedge against unexpected market downturns.

19. C is correct. Xu states that she prefers opportunistic hedge fund strategies that use high leverage, have high liquidity, and exhibit right-tail skewness. The two most common opportunistic hedge fund strategies are global macro and managed futures. Both global macro and managed futures are highly liquid. Further, returns of managed futures strategies typically exhibit positive right-tail skewness in periods of market stress, whereas global macro strategies have delivered similar diversification in such stress periods but with more heterogeneous outcomes. Global macro and managed futures strategies can also use high leverage, either through the use of futures contracts, in which high leverage is embedded, or through the active use of options, which adds natural elements of leverage and positive convexity.

   A and B are incorrect because both global macro and managed futures strategies can offer the three characteristics that Xu seeks in an opportunistic hedge fund strategy.

20. B is correct. Xu bought 22,500 shares of Taurus at €20 per share for a total cost of €450,000 and sold short 15,000 shares of Aqua at €45 per share for a total cost of €675,000. Given the offer ratio of two shares of Aqua for three shares of Taurus, the 22,500 shares of Taurus are economically equivalent to 15,000 shares of Aqua. Thus, assuming the deal closes, the payoff to Xu's trade is €675,000 − €450,000 = €225,000.

   A is incorrect because −€187,500 is the payoff if the merger fails and both companies' share prices revert back to their pre-merger prices. Xu bought 22,500 shares of Taurus at €20 per share for a total cost of €450,000 and sold short 15,000 shares of Aqua at €45 per share for a total cost of €675,000. If the merger fails and the share prices revert back to pre-announcement levels, Xu will have to sell 22,500 shares of Taurus at €15 per share for proceeds of €337,500, resulting in a loss on the Taurus stock of −€112,500 (€337,500 − €450,000). Xu will also have to close the short position by purchasing 15,000 shares of Aqua at €50 per share for a total cost of €750,000. This will result in a loss on Aqua of −€75,000 (€675,000 − €750,000). The total loss is −€112,500 + −€75,000 = −€187,500.

   C is incorrect because the initial pre-merger prices are used to compute the payoff: 22,500 shares of Taurus are bought for €15 per share for a total of €337,500, and 15,000 shares of Aqua are sold short at €50 per share for a total of €750,000. The payoff is €750,000 − €337,500 = €412,500.

21. C is correct. Xu's decision to short ZMD and take a long position in Tarreras with equal beta-weighted exposure is an example of a pairs trade or an equity-market-neutral strategy. Xu is neutralizing market risk by constructing a strategy where the expected portfolio beta is zero. Since her strategy does not take beta risk and attempts to neutralize many other factor risks, Xu must apply leverage to the long and short positions to achieve a meaningful expected return from the stock selection.

    A is incorrect because in a short-biased hedge fund strategy, the manager aims to sell expensively priced equities but may balance the short exposure with some modest long exposure. Xu, however, has entered into an equity-market-neutral pairs trade that takes opposite long and short positions in an attempt to eliminate market exposure. Her positions do not have a short bias.

    B is incorrect because long/short equity managers buy equities of companies they expect will rise and sell short equities of companies they believe will fall in value. When long and short positions are placed together into a portfolio, the market exposure is the net of the beta-adjusted long and short exposures; however, the target beta is typically not zero. Xu is neutralizing market risk by constructing a strategy where the expected portfolio beta is zero.

22. A is correct. The classic convertible bond arbitrage strategy is to buy the relatively undervalued convertible bond and take a short position in the relatively overvalued underlying stock. If the convertible bond's current price is near the conversion value, then the combination of a long convertible and short equity delta exposure will create a situation where for small changes in the share price and ignoring dividends and borrowing costs, the profit/loss will be the same.

    The current conversion price of the AVC convertible bond is €1,000 × (115/100)/50 = €23, and the current AVC share price is €28. Thus, by purchasing the convertible bond, selling short the shares, exercising the conversion option, and selling the shares at the current market price, a profit of €5 can be locked in regardless of changes in the share price. The following table demonstrates this result by showing the same trade profit of €5 for three different stock prices:

AVC New Share Price	Profit on: Long Stock via Convertible Bond at $23/Sh.	Short Stock at $28/Sh.	Total Profit
€26	€3	€2	**€5**
€28	€5	€0	**€5**
€34	€11	–€6	**€5**

where

Long stock via convertible bond profit = New share price – Current conversion price
Short stock profit = Current share price – New share price
Total profit = Long stock via convertible bond profit + Short stock profit

Thus, regardless of the share price, the total profit on the convertible arbitrage trade is €5.

B is incorrect because if the convertible bond's current price is near the conversion value, then the combination of a long convertible and short equity delta exposure will create a situation where the profit/loss will be the same (not higher if the share price decreases).

C is incorrect because if the convertible bond's current price is near the conversion value, then the combination of a long convertible and short equity delta exposure will create a situation where for small changes in equity price, the profit/loss will be the same (not higher if the share price increases).

23. B is correct. Hedge funds look for policies in which the ongoing premium payments to keep the policy active are relatively low, so Characteristic 2 is correct. Hedge funds also look for life settlements where the surrender value offered to the insured individual is also relatively low and the probability that the designated insured person is likely to die earlier than predicted by standard actuarial methods is relatively high.

A is incorrect because hedge funds look for policies in which the surrender value offered to the insured individual is relatively low (not high) in order to enhance return by purchasing at a lower price.

C is incorrect because hedge funds look for settlements in which the probability that the designated insured person is likely to die *earlier* than predicted by standard actuarial methods is relatively high. This means the hedge fund's cash outflows to pay the ongoing premium will be less than predicted, which will enhance return.

CAPITAL MARKET EXPECTATIONS: FORECASTING ASSET CLASS RETURNS

LEARNING OUTCOMES

The candidate should be able to:

- discuss approaches to setting expectations for fixed-income returns;
- discuss risks faced by investors in emerging market fixed-income securities and the country risk analysis techniques used to evaluate emerging market economies;
- discuss approaches to setting expectations for equity investment market returns;
- discuss risks faced by investors in emerging market equity securities;
- explain how economic and competitive factors can affect expectations for real estate investment markets and sector returns;
- discuss major approaches to forecasting exchange rates;
- discuss methods of forecasting volatility;
- recommend and justify changes in the component weights of a global investment portfolio based on trends and expected changes in macroeconomic factors.

SUMMARY OVERVIEW

The following are the main points covered in the reading.

- The choice among forecasting techniques is effectively a choice of the information on which forecasts will be conditioned and how that information will be incorporated into the forecasts.
- The formal forecasting tools most commonly used in forecasting capital market returns fall into three broad categories: statistical methods, discounted cash flow models, and risk premium models.
- Sample statistics, especially the sample mean, are subject to substantial estimation error.
- Shrinkage estimation combines two estimates (or sets of estimates) into a more precise estimate.
- Time-series estimators, which explicitly incorporate dynamics, may summarize historical data well without providing insight into the underlying drivers of forecasts.
- Discounted cash flow models are used to estimate the required return implied by an asset's current price.
- The risk premium approach expresses expected return as the sum of the risk-free rate of interest and one or more risk premiums.
- There are three methods for modeling risk premiums: equilibrium models, such as the CAPM; factor models; and building blocks.
- The DCF method is the only one that is precise enough to use in support of trades involving individual fixed-income securities.
- There are three main methods for developing expected returns for fixed-income asset classes: DCF, building blocks, and inclusion in an equilibrium model.
- As a forecast of bond return, YTM, the most commonly quoted metric, can be improved by incorporating the impact of yield changes on reinvestment of cash flows and valuation at the investment horizon.
- The building blocks for fixed-income expected returns are the short-term default-free rate, the term premium, the credit premium, and the liquidity premium.
- Term premiums are roughly proportional to duration, whereas credit premiums tend to be larger at the short end of the curve.
- Both term premiums and credit premiums are positively related to the slope of the yield curve.
- Credit spreads reflect both the credit premium (i.e., additional expected return) and expected losses due to default.
- A baseline estimate of the liquidity premium can be based on the yield spread between the highest-quality issuer in a market (usually the sovereign) and the next highest-quality large issuer (often a government agency).
- Emerging market debt exposes investors to heightened risk with respect to both ability to pay and willingness to pay, which can be associated with the economy and political/legal weaknesses, respectively.
- The Grinold–Kroner model decomposes the expected return on equities into three components: (1) expected cash flow return, composed of the dividend yield minus the rate of change in shares outstanding, (2) expected return due to nominal earnings growth, and (3) expected repricing return, reflecting the rate of change in the P/E.
- Forecasting the equity premium directly is just as difficult as projecting the absolute level of equity returns, so the building block approach provides little, if any, specific insight with which to improve equity return forecasts.

- The Singer–Terhaar version of the international capital asset pricing model combines a global CAPM equilibrium that assumes full market integration with expected returns for each asset class based on complete segmentation.

- Emerging market equities expose investors to the same underlying risks as emerging market debt does: more fragile economies, less stable political and policy frameworks, and weaker legal protections.

- Emerging market investors need to pay particular attention to the ways in which the value of their ownership claims might be expropriated. Among the areas of concern are standards of corporate governance, accounting and disclosure standards, property rights laws, and checks and balances on governmental actions.

- Historical return data for real estate is subject to substantial smoothing, which biases standard volatility estimates downward and distorts correlations with other asset classes. Meaningful analysis of real estate as an asset class requires explicit handling of this data issue.

- Real estate is subject to boom–bust cycles that both drive and are driven by the business cycle.

- The cap rate, defined as net operating income in the current period divided by the property value, is the standard valuation metric for commercial real estate.

- A model similar to the Grinold–Kroner model can be applied to estimate the expected return on real estate:

$$E(R_{re}) = \text{Cap rate} + \text{NOI growth rate} - \%\Delta\text{Cap rate}.$$

- There is a clear pattern of higher cap rates for riskier property types, lower-quality properties, and less attractive locations.

- Real estate expected returns contain all the standard building block risk premiums:

  - Term premium: As a very long-lived asset with relatively stable cash flows, income-producing real estate has a high duration.

  - Credit premium: A fixed-term lease is like a corporate bond issued by the leaseholder and secured by the property.

  - Equity premium: Owners bear the risk of property value fluctuations, as well as risk associated with rent growth, lease renewal, and vacancies.

  - Liquidity premium: Real estate trades infrequently and is costly to transact.

- Currency exchange rates are especially difficult to forecast because they are tied to governments, financial systems, legal systems, and geographies. Forecasting exchange rates requires identification and assessment of the forces that are likely to exert the most influence.

- Provided they can be financed, trade flows do not usually exert a significant impact on exchange rates. International capital flows are typically larger and more volatile than trade-financing flows.

- PPP is a poor predictor of exchange rate movements over short to intermediate horizons but is a better guide to currency movements over progressively longer multi-year horizons.

- The extent to which the current account balance influences the exchange rate depends primarily on whether it is likely to be persistent and, if so, whether it can be sustained.

- Capital seeks the highest risk-adjusted expected return. In a world of perfect capital mobility, in the long run, the exchange rate will be driven to the point at which the expected percentage change equals the "excess" risk-adjusted expected return on the portfolio of assets denominated in the domestic currency over that of the portfolio of assets denominated in the foreign currency. However, in the short run, there can be an exchange rate overshoot in the opposite direction as hot money chases higher returns.

- Carry trades are profitable on average, which is contrary to the predictions of uncovered interest rate parity.
- Each country/currency has a unique portfolio of assets that makes up part of the global "market portfolio." Exchange rates provide an across-the-board mechanism for adjusting the relative sizes of these portfolios to match investors' desire to hold them.
- The portfolio balance perspective implies that exchange rates adjust in response to changes in the relative sizes and compositions of the aggregate portfolios denominated in each currency.
- The sample variance–covariance matrix is an unbiased estimate of the true VCV structure; that is, it will be correct on average.
- There are two main problems with using the sample VCV matrix as an estimate/forecast of the true VCV matrix: It cannot be used for large numbers of asset classes, and it is subject to substantial sampling error.
- Linear factor models impose structure on the VCV matrix that allows them to handle very large numbers of asset classes. The drawback is that the VCV matrix is biased and inconsistent unless the assumed structure is true.
- Shrinkage estimation of the VCV matrix is a weighted average of the sample VCV matrix and a target VCV matrix that reflects assumed "prior" knowledge of the true VCV structure.
- Failure to adjust for the impact of smoothing in observed return data for real estate and other private assets will almost certainly lead to distorted portfolio analysis and hence poor asset allocation decisions.
- Financial asset returns exhibit volatility clustering, evidenced by periods of high and low volatilities. ARCH models were developed to address these time-varying volatilities.
- One of the simplest and most used ARCH models represents today's variance as a linear combination of yesterday's variance and a new "shock" to volatility. With appropriate parameter values, the model exhibits the volatility clustering characteristic of financial asset returns.

PROBLEMS

1. An investor is considering adding three new securities to her internationally focused fixed income portfolio. She considers the following non-callable securities:
   - 1-year government bond
   - 10-year government bond
   - 10-year BBB rated corporate bond

   She plans to invest equally in all three securities being analyzed or will invest in none of them at this time. She will only make the added investment provided that the expected spread/premium of the equally weighted investment is at least 1.5 percent (150bp) over the 1-year government bond. She has gathered the following information:

Risk free interest rate (1-year, incorporating 2.6% inflation expectation)	3.8%
Term premium (10-year vs. 1-year government bond)	1%
10-year BBB credit premium (over 10-year government bond)	75bp
Estimated liquidity premium on 10-year corporate bonds	55bp

Using only the information given, address the following problems using the risk premium approach:

A. Calculate the expected return that an equal-weighted investment in the three securities could provide.

B. Calculate the expected total risk premium of the three securities and determine the investor's probable course of action.

2. Jo Akumba's portfolio is invested in a range of developed markets fixed income securities. She asks her adviser about the possibility of diversifying her investments to include emerging and frontier markets government and corporate fixed income securities. Her adviser makes the following comment regarding risk:

> *All emerging and frontier market fixed income securities pose economic, political and legal risk. Economic risks arise from the fact that emerging market countries have poor fiscal discipline, rely on foreign borrowing, have less diverse tax base and significant dependence on specific industries. They are susceptible to capital flight. Their ability to pay is limited. In addition, weak property rights, weak enforcement of contract laws and political instability pose hazard for emerging markets debt investors.*

> *Discuss the statement made.*

3. An Australian investor currently holds a A$240 million equity portfolio. He is considering rebalancing the portfolio based on an assessment of the risk and return prospects facing the Australian economy. Information relating to the Australian investment markets and the economy has been collected in the following table:

10-Year Historical	Current	Capital Market Expectations
Average government bond yield: 2.8%	10-year government bond yield: 2.3%	
Average annual equity return: 4.6%	Year-over-year equity return: −9.4%	
Average annual inflation rate: 2.3%	Year-over-year inflation rate: 2.1%	Expected annual inflation: 2.3%
Equity market P/E (beginning of period): 15×	Current equity market P/E: 14.5×	Expected equity market P/E: 14.0×
Average annual dividend income return: 2.6%		Expected annual income return: 2.4%
Average annual real earnings growth: 6.0%		Expected annual real earnings growth: 5.0%

Using the information in the table, address the following problems:

A. Calculate the historical Australian equity risk premium using the "equity-vs-bonds" premium method.
B. Calculate the expected annual equity return using the Grinold–Kroner model (assume no change in the number of shares outstanding).
C. Using your answer to Part B, calculate the expected annual equity risk premium.

4. An analyst is reviewing various asset alternatives and is presented with the following information relating to the broad equity market of Switzerland and various industries within the Swiss market that are of particular investment interest.

Expected risk premium for overall global investable market (GIM) portfolio	3.5%
Expected standard deviation for the GIM portfolio	8.5%
Expected standard deviation for Swiss Healthcare Industry equity investments	12.0%
Expected standard deviation for Swiss Watch Industry equity investments	6.0%
Expected standard deviation for Swiss Consumer Products Industry equity investments	7.5%

Assume that the Swiss market is perfectly integrated with the world markets.
Swiss Healthcare has a correlation of 0.7 with the GIM portfolio.
Swiss Watch has a correlation of 0.8 with the GIM portfolio.
Swiss Consumer Products has a correlation of 0.8 with the GIM portfolio.

A. Basing your answers only upon the data presented in the table above and using the international capital asset pricing model—in particular, the Singer–Terhaar approach—estimate the expected risk premium for the following:
   i)   Swiss Health Care Industry
   ii) Swiss Watch Industry
   iii) Swiss Consumer Products Industry
B. Judge which industry is most attractive from a valuation perspective.

5. Identify risks faced by investors in emerging market equities over and above those that are faced by fixed income investors in such markets.

6. Describe the main issues that arise when conducting historical analysis of real estate returns.

7. An analyst at a real estate investment management firm seeks to establish expectations for rate of return for properties in the industrial sector over the next year. She has obtained the following information:

Current industrial sector capitalization rate ("cap" rate)	5.7%
Expected cap rate at the end of the period	5.5%
NOI growth rate (real)	1%
Inflation expectation	1.5%

Estimate the expected return from the industrial sector properties based on the data provided.

8. A client has asked his adviser to explain the key considerations in forecasting exchange rates. The adviser's firm uses two broad complementary approaches when setting expectations for exchange rate movements, namely focus on trade in goods and services and, secondly, focus on capital flows. Identify the main considerations that the adviser should explain to the client under the two approaches.

9. Looking independently at each of the economic observations below, indicate the country where an analyst would expect to see a strengthening currency for each observation.

	Country X	Country Y
Expected inflation over next year	2.0%	3.0%
Short-term (1-month) government rate	Decrease	Increase
Expected (forward-looking) GDP growth over next year	2.0%	3.3%
New national laws have been passed that enable foreign direct investment in real estate/financial companies	Yes	No
Current account surplus (deficit)	8%	−1%

10. Fap is a small country whose currency is the Fip. Three years ago, the exchange rate was considered to be reflecting purchasing power parity (PPP). Since then, the country's inflation has exceeded inflation in the other countries by about 5% per annum. The Fip exchange rate, however, remained broadly unchanged.

   What would you have expected the Fip exchange rate to show if PPP prevailed? Are Fips over or undervalued, according to PPP?

The following information relates to Questions 11–18.

Richard Martin is chief investment officer for the Trunch Foundation (the foundation), which has a large, globally diversified investment portfolio. Martin meets with the foundation's fixed-income and real estate portfolio managers to review expected return forecasts and potential investments, as well as to consider short-term modifications to asset weights within the total fund strategic asset allocation.

Martin asks the real estate portfolio manager to discuss the performance characteristics of real estate. The real estate portfolio manager makes the following statements:

Statement 1: Adding traded REIT securities to an equity portfolio should substantially improve the portfolio's diversification over the next year.

Statement 2: Traded REIT securities are more highly correlated with direct real estate and less highly correlated with equities over multi-year horizons.

Martin looks over the long-run valuation metrics the manager is using for commercial real estate, shown in Exhibit 1.

EXHIBIT 1 Commercial Real Estate Valuation Metrics

Cap Rate	GDP Growth Rate
4.70%	4.60%

The real estate team uses an in-house model for private real estate to estimate the true volatility of returns over time. The model assumes that the current observed return equals the weighted average of the current true return and the previous observed return. Because the true return is not observable, the model assumes a relationship between true returns and observable REIT index returns; therefore, it uses REIT index returns as proxies for both the unobservable current true return and the previous observed return.

Martin asks the fixed-income portfolio manager to review the foundation's bond portfolios. The existing aggregate bond portfolio is broadly diversified in domestic and international developed markets. The first segment of the portfolio to be reviewed is the domestic sovereign portfolio. The bond manager notes that there is a market consensus that the domestic yield curve will likely experience a single 20 bp increase in the near term as a result of monetary tightening and then remain relatively flat and stable for the next three years. Martin then reviews duration and yield measures for the short-term domestic sovereign bond portfolio in Exhibit 2.

EXHIBIT 2   Short-Term Domestic Sovereign Bond Portfolio

Macaulay Duration	Modified Duration	Yield to Maturity
3.00	2.94	2.00%

The discussion turns to the international developed fixed-income market. The foundation invested in bonds issued by Country XYZ, a foreign developed country. XYZ's sovereign yield curve is currently upward sloping, and the yield spread between 2-year and 10-year XYZ bonds is 100 bps.

The fixed-income portfolio manager tells Martin that he is interested in a domestic market corporate bond issued by Zeus Manufacturing Corporation (ZMC). ZMC has just been downgraded two steps by a major credit rating agency. In addition to expected monetary actions that will raise short-term rates, the yield spread between three-year sovereign bonds and the next highest-quality government agency bond widened by 10 bps.

Although the foundation's fixed-income portfolios have focused primarily on developed markets, the portfolio manager presents data in Exhibit 3 on two emerging markets for Martin to consider. Both economies increased exports of their mineral resources over the last decade.

EXHIBIT 3   Emerging Market Data

Factor	Emerging Republic A	Emerging Republic B
Fiscal deficit/GDP	6.50%	8.20%
Debt/GDP	90.10%	104.20%
Current account deficit	5.20% of GDP	7.10% of GDP
Foreign exchange reserves	90.30% of short-term debt	70.10% of short-term debt

The fixed-income portfolio manager also presents information on a new investment opportunity in an international developed market. The team is considering the bonds of Xdelp, a large energy exploration and production company. Both the domestic and international markets are experiencing synchronized growth in GDP midway between the trough and the peak of the business cycle. The foreign country's government has displayed a disciplined approach to maintaining stable monetary and fiscal policies and has experienced a rising current account surplus and an appreciating currency. It is expected that with the improvements in free cash flow and earnings, the credit rating of the Xdelp bonds will be upgraded. Martin refers to the foundation's asset allocation policy in Exhibit 4 before making any changes to either the fixed-income or real estate portfolios.

EXHIBIT 4   Trunch Foundation Strategic Asset Allocation—Select Data

Asset Class	Minimum Weight	Maximum Weight	Actual Weight
Fixed income—Domestic	40.00%	80.00%	43.22%
Fixed income—International	5.00%	10.00%	6.17%
Fixed income—Emerging markets	0.00%	2.00%	0.00%
Alternatives—Real estate	2.00%	6.00%	3.34%

11. Which of the real estate portfolio manager's statements is correct?
    A. Only Statement 1
    B. Only Statement 2
    C. Both Statement 1 and Statement 2
12. Based only on Exhibit 1, the long-run expected return for commercial real estate:
    A. is approximately double the cap rate.
    B. incorporates a cap rate greater than the discount rate.
    C. needs to include the cap rate's anticipated rate of change.
13. Based on the private real estate model developed to estimate return volatility, the true variance is *most likely*:
    A. lower than the variance of the observed data.
    B. approximately equal to the variance of the observed data.
    C. greater than the variance of the observed data.
14. Based on Exhibit 2 and the anticipated effects of the monetary policy change, the expected annual return over a three-year investment horizon will *most likely* be:
    A. lower than 2.00%.
    B. approximately equal to 2.00%.
    C. greater than 2.00%.
15. Based on the building block approach to fixed-income returns, the dominant source of the yield spread for Country XYZ is *most likely* the:
    A. term premium.
    B. credit premium.
    C. liquidity premium.
16. Using the building block approach, the required rate of return for the ZMC bond will *most likely*:
    A. increase based on the change in the credit premium.
    B. decrease based on the change in the default-free rate.
    C. decrease based on the change in the liquidity premium.
17. Based only on Exhibit 3, the foundation would *most likely* consider buying bonds issued by:
    A. only Emerging Republic A.
    B. only Emerging Republic B.
    C. neither Emerging Republic A nor Emerging Republic B.
18. Based only on Exhibits 3 and 4 and the information provided by the portfolio managers, the action *most likely* to enhance returns is to:
    A. decrease existing investments in real estate by 2.00%.
    B. initiate a commitment to emerging market debt of 1.00%.
    C. increase the investments in international market bonds by 1.00%.

The following information relates to Questions 19–26.

Judith Bader is a senior analyst for a company that specializes in managing international developed and emerging markets equities. Next week, Bader must present proposed changes to client portfolios to the Investment Committee, and she is preparing a presentation to support the views underlying her recommendations.

Bader begins by analyzing portfolio risk. She decides to forecast a variance–covariance matrix (VCV) for 20 asset classes, using 10 years of monthly returns and incorporating both the sample statistics and the factor-model methods. To mitigate the impact of estimation error, Bader is considering combining the results of the two methods in an alternative target VCV matrix, using shrinkage estimation.

Bader asks her research assistant to comment on the two approaches and the benefits of applying shrinkage estimation. The assistant makes the following statements:

Statement 1:   Shrinkage estimation of VCV matrices will decrease the efficiency of the estimates versus the sample VCV matrix.

Statement 2:   Your proposed approach for estimating the VCV matrix will not be reliable because a sample VCV matrix is biased and inconsistent.

Statement 3:   A factor-based VCV matrix approach may result in some portfolios that erroneously appear to be riskless if any asset returns can be completely determined by the common factors or some of the factors are redundant.

Bader then uses the Singer–Terhaar model and the final shrinkage-estimated VCV matrix to determine the equilibrium expected equity returns for all international asset classes by country. Three of the markets under consideration are located in Country A (developed market), Country B (emerging market), and Country C (emerging market). Bader projects that in relation to the global market, the equity market in Country A will remain highly integrated, the equity market in Country B will become more segmented, and the equity market in Country C will become more fully integrated.

Next, Bader applies the Grinold–Kroner model to estimate the expected equity returns for the various markets under consideration. For Country A, Bader assumes a very long-term corporate earnings growth rate of 4% per year (equal to the expected nominal GDP growth rate), a 2% rate of net share repurchases for Country A's equities, and an expansion rate for P/E multiples of 0.5% per year.

In reviewing Countries B and C, Bader's research assistant comments that emerging markets are especially risky owing to issues related to politics, competition, and accounting standards. As an example, Bader and her assistant discuss the risk implications of the following information related to Country B:

* Experiencing declining per capita income
* Expected to continue its persistent current account deficit below 2% of GDP
* Transitioning to International Financial Reporting Standards, with full convergence scheduled to be completed within two years

Bader shifts her focus to currency expectations relative to clients' base currency and summarizes her assumptions in Exhibit 5.

EXHIBIT 5   Baseline Assumptions for Currency Forecasts

	Country A	Country B	Country C
Historical current account	Persistent current account deficit of 5% of GDP	Persistent current account deficit of 2% of GDP	Persistent current account surplus of 2% of GDP
Expectation for secular trend in current account	Rising current account deficit	Narrowing current account deficit	Rising current account surplus
Long-term inflation expectation relative to global inflation	Expected to rise	Expected to keep pace	Expected to fall
Capital flows	Steady inflows	Hot money flowing out	Hot money flowing in

During a conversation about Exhibit 1, Bader and her research assistant discuss the composition of each country's currency portfolio and the potential for triggering a crisis. Bader notes that some flows and holdings are more or less supportive of the currency, stating that investments in private equity make up the majority of Country A's currency portfolio, investments in public equity make up the majority of Country B's currency portfolio, and investments in public debt make up the majority of Country C's currency portfolio.

19. Which of the following statements made by Bader's research assistant is correct?
    A. Statement 1
    B. Statement 2
    C. Statement 3
20. Based on expectations for changes in integration with the global market, all else being equal, the Singer–Terhaar model implies that Bader should shift capital from Country A to:
    A. only Country B.
    B. only Country C.
    C. both Countries B and C.
21. Using the Grinold–Kroner model, which of the following assumptions for forecasting Country A's expected equity returns is plausible for the very long run?
    A. Rate of net share repurchases
    B. Corporate earnings growth rate
    C. Expansion rate for P/E multiples
22. Based only on the emerging markets discussion, developments in which of the following areas *most likely* signal increasing risk for Country B's equity market?
    A. Politics
    B. Competitiveness
    C. Accounting standards
23. Based on Bader's expectations for current account secular trends as shown in Exhibit 5, Bader should reallocate capital, all else being equal, from:
    A. Country A to Country C.
    B. Country B to Country A.
    C. Country C to Country A.

24. Based on Bader's inflation expectations as shown in Exhibit 5, purchasing power parity implies that which of the following countries' currencies should depreciate, all else being equal?
    A. Country A
    B. Country B
    C. Country C

25. Based on Exhibit 5, which country's central bank is *most likely* to buy domestic bonds near term to sterilize the impact of money flows on domestic liquidity?
    A. Country A
    B. Country B
    C. Country C

26. Based on the composition of each country's currency portfolio, which country is most vulnerable to a potential crisis?
    A. Country A
    B. Country B
    C. Country C

CAPITAL MARKET EXPECTATIONS: FORECASTING ASSET CLASS RETURNS

SOLUTIONS

1.
   A.

	Risk free interest rate (nominal) (%)	+	Premiums (%)	=	Expected annual fixed-income return (%)
1-year government bond	3.8	+	0	=	3.8
10-year government bond	3.8	+	1	=	4.8
10-year corporate bond	3.8	+	1 + 0.75 + 0.55	=	6.1

   Estimate of the expected return of an equal-weighted investment in the three securities: (3.8% + 4.8% + 6.1%)/3 = 4.9%.

   B. The average spread (over 1-year government bond) at issue is [0 + 1 + (1 + 0.75 + 0.55)] = 3.3%/3 = 1.1%.

   As the 1.1% is less than 1.5%, the investor will not make the investment.

2. The statement correctly identifies economic, political and legal risk. The adviser has correctly identified some of the characteristics typically associated with emerging and frontier markets that may affect their governments' and corporate borrowers' ability and willingness to pay bondholders. However, the assertion that all emerging and frontier market fixed income securities pose such risk is incorrect, as many countries classified as "emerging" are considered to be healthy and prosperous economies.

3.

    A. The historical equity risk premium is 1.8%, calculated as follows:
       Historical equity returns − Historical 10-year government bond yield = Historical
       equity risk premium

$$4.6\% - 2.8\% = 1.8\%$$

    B. The Grinold–Kroner model states that the expected return on equity is the sum of the
       expected income return (2.4%), the expected nominal earnings growth return (7.3%
       = 2.3% from inflation + 5.0% from real earnings growth) and the expected repricing
       return (−3.45%). The expected change in market valuation of −3.45 is calculated
       as the percentage change in the P/E level from the current 14.5× to the expected level
       of 14.0×: (14 − 14.5)/14.5 = −3.45%. Thus, the expected return is 2.4% + 7.3% −
       3.45% = 6.25%.
    C. Using the results from Part B, the expected equity return is 6.25 percent.

       Expected equity return − Current 10-year government bond yield = Expected equity
                                                             risk premium

$$6.25\% - 2.3\% = 3.95\%.$$

4.

    A. Using the formula $RP_i^G = \rho_{i,GM} \sigma_i \left(\dfrac{RP_{GM}}{\sigma_{GM}} \right)$ we can solve for each expected industry
       risk premium. The term in brackets is the Sharpe ratio for the GIM, computed as
       3.5/8.5 = 0.412.
       i) $RP_{\text{Healthcare}} = (12)(0.7)(0.412) = 3.46\%$
       ii) $RP_{\text{Watch}} = (6)(0.8)(0.412) = 1.98\%$
       iii) $RP_{\text{Consumer Products}} = (7.5)(0.8)(0.412) = 2.47\%$
    B. Based on the above analysis, the Swiss Healthcare Industry would have the highest
       expected return. However, that expected return reflects compensation for systematic
       risk. Based on the data provided we cannot conclude which industry is most attractive
       from a valuation standpoint.

5. In addition to the economic, political and legal risks faced by fixed income investors,
   equity investors in emerging markets face corporate governance risks. Their ownership
   claims may be expropriated by corporate insiders, dominant shareholders or the government. Interested parties may misuse the companies' assets. Weak disclosure and accounting standards may result in limited transparency that favors insiders. Weak checks and
   balances on governmental actions may bring about regulatory uncertainty, seizure of
   property or nationalization.

6. Properties trade infrequently so there is no data on simultaneous periodic transaction
   prices for a selection of properties. Analysis therefore relies on appraisals. Secondly, each
   property is different, it is said to be heterogenous. The returns calculated from appraisals
   represent weighted averages of unobservable returns. Published return series is too smooth
   and the sample volatility understates the true volatility of returns. It also distorts estimates
   of correlations.

7. The expected change in the cap rate from 5.7% to 5.5% represents a (5.5% − 5.7%)/5.7%
   = 3.5% decrease.

      Using the expression $E(R_{re})$ = CapRate + NOI growth rate − %ΔCapRate = 5.7% +
   (1% + 1.5%) − (−3.5%) = 11.7%.

Note: As the cap rate is expected to decrease, property values are expected to increase, hence the cap
rate change contributes to the expected return.

8. Under the first approach analysts focus on flows of export and imports to establish what the net trade flows are and how large they are relative to the economy and other, potentially larger financing and investment flows. The approach also considers differences between domestic and foreign inflation rates that relate to the concept of purchasing power parity. Under PPP, the expected percentage change in the exchange rate should equal the difference between inflation rates. The approach also considers the sustainability of current account imbalances, reflecting the difference between national saving and investment.

   Under the second approach the analysis focuses on capital flows and the degree of capital mobility. It assumes that capital seeks the highest risk-adjusted return. The expected changes in the exchange rate will reflect the differences in the respective countries' assets' characteristics such as relative short-term interest rates, term, credit, equity and liquidity premiums. The approach also considers hot money flows and the fact that exchange rates provide an across the board mechanism for adjusting the relative sizes of each country's portfolio of assets.

9.

	Country X	Country Y
Expected inflation over next year	2.0%	3.0%
Short-term (1-month) government rate	Decrease	Increase
Expected (forward-looking) GDP growth over next year	2.0%	3.3%
New national laws have been passed that enable foreign direct investment in real estate/financial companies	Yes	No
Current account surplus (deficit)	8%	−1%

Note: The shaded cells represent the comparatively stronger measure, where an analyst could expect to see a strengthening currency based on the factor being independently reviewed.

10. According to PPP, to offset the effect of the higher inflation in Fap, the Fip should have depreciated against the other currencies by approximately the difference between Fap inflation and that in the other countries.

   According to PPP, Fip is overvalued.

11. B is correct. Statement 2 is correct because traded REIT securities are more highly correlated with direct real estate and less highly correlated with equities over multi-year horizons. Thus, although REITs tend to act like stocks in the short run, they act like real estate in the longer run.

   A and C are incorrect because Statement 1 is not correct. Traded REIT securities have relatively high correlations with equity securities over short time horizons, such as one year. The higher correlations suggest that traded REIT securities will not act as a good diversifier for an equity portfolio over a one-year period.

12. A is correct. An estimate of the long-run expected or required return for commercial real estate equals the sum of the capitalization rate (cap rate) plus the growth rate (constant) of net operating income (NOI). An approximation of the steady-state NOI growth rate for commercial real estate is equal to the growth rate in GDP. Thus, from Equation 7.7 and the information provided in Exhibit P7.1, $E(R_{re})$ = Cap rate + NOI growth rate = 4.70% + 4.60% = 9.30%, which is approximately double the cap rate.

   B is incorrect because the discount rate (expected or required return) equals the sum of the cap rate and the NOI growth rate. Based on the information in Exhibit P7.1, the 4.70% cap rate is less than (not greater than) the 9.30% discount rate.

C is incorrect because the discount rate over finite horizons (not long-run horizons) needs to include the anticipated rate of change in the cap rate. For long-run expected return calculations, the anticipated rate of change in the cap rate is not included.

13. C is correct. The in-house model assumes that the current observed return equals the weighted average of the current true return and the previous observed return. The model uses REIT index returns as proxies for the returns in the model. The smoothed nature of most published (observed) real estate returns is a major contributor to the appearance of low correlation with financial assets. This smoothing dampens the volatility of the observed data and distorts correlations with other assets. Thus, the raw observable data tend to understate the risk and overstate the diversification benefits of these asset classes. It is generally accepted that the true variance of real estate returns is greater than the variance of the observed data.

14. B is correct. If the investment horizon equals the (Macaulay) duration of the portfolio, the capital loss created by the increase in yields and the reinvestment effects (gains) will roughly offset, leaving the realized return approximately equal to the original yield to maturity. This relationship is exact if: (a) the yield curve is flat and (b) the change in rates occurs immediately in a single step. In practice, the relationship is only an approximation. In the case of the domestic sovereign yield curve, the 20 bp increase in rates will likely be offset by the higher reinvestment rate, creating an annual return approximately equal to 2.00%.

15. A is correct. From the building block approach to fixed-income returns, the required return for fixed-income asset classes has four components: the one-period default-free rate, the term premium, the credit premium, and the liquidity premium. Since sovereign bonds are considered the highest-quality bonds, they likely do not have a significant credit premium nor are they likely to have a significant premium for illiquidity. The slope of the yield curve is useful information on which to base forecasts of the term premium. Therefore, the dominant source of the yield spread is most likely the term premium for XYZ's sovereign bond.

16. A is correct. The credit premium is the additional expected return demanded for bearing the risk of default losses. A credit downgrade two steps lower will increase the credit premium and the required rate of return. The change in the default-free rate associated with the monetary tightening will increase (not decrease) the required rate of return. The widening of the spread between the sovereign bond and the next highest-quality government agency security indicates an increase in the liquidity premium, which will increase (not decrease) the required rate of return.

B is incorrect because the required rate of return would increase (not decrease) based on the change in the default-free rate associated with the monetary tightening.

C is incorrect because the rate of return would increase (not decrease) based on a change in the liquidity premium. The liquidity premium can be estimated from the yield spread between the highest-quality issuer (typically a sovereign bond) and the next highest-quality large issuer of similar bonds (often a government agency). A widening yield spread indicates an increase in the liquidity premium and required rate of return.

17. C is correct. Emerging market debt requires an analysis of economic and political/legal risks. Based on the macroeconomic factors, the risk of a bond investment in either Republic A or Republic B appears to be high. Thresholds such as the risk guidelines listed in the table below can be used to assess the attractiveness of the two emerging market (EM) opportunities in Republic A and Republic B. Most notably, both republics raise concern

based solely on their fiscal deficit-to-GDP ratios greater than 4.00% (Republic A's is 6.50% and Republic B's is 8.20%).

EMERGING MARKET ANALYSIS

Country Political/Economic Risk	Emerging Market Risk Guidelines	Emerging Republic A	Emerging Republic B
Fiscal deficit/GDP	4.00%	Negative	Negative
Debt/GDP	70.00%	Negative	Negative
Current account deficit	4.00% of GDP	Negative	Negative
Foreign exchange reserves	100.00% of short-term debt	Negative	Negative

Analysis of the economic and political risks associated with the two EM opportunities is suggestive of the need for further scrutiny; therefore, the foundation should not invest in Emerging Republic A or Emerging Republic B based only on the information provided.

18. C is correct. An investment in the bonds of the international energy exploration and production company (Xdelp) looks attractive. The international market benefits from positive macroeconomic fundamentals: point in the business cycle, monetary and fiscal discipline, rising current account surplus, and an appreciating currency. The anticipated credit rating improvement will add to the potential for this to become a profitable investment and enhance returns. An increase in the investments within the international fixed-income segment by 1.00% (existing weight is 6.17%) would take advantage of this opportunity and remain in compliance with the foundation's 5.00%–10.00% strategic asset allocation limits.

A is incorrect because a decrease in the existing weight of real estate by 2.00% would put the portfolio weight below the minimum threshold of 2.00% (i.e., 3.34% − 2.00% = 1.34%) of the foundation's strategic asset allocation.

B is incorrect because the information presented in Exhibit P7.3 would lead the chief investment officer to avoid the two opportunities in emerging market debt (Emerging Republic A and Emerging Republic B) and not initiate a commitment to emerging market debt of 1.00% (i.e., increase the existing weight above 0.00%).

19. C is correct. Statement 3 is correct. As long as none of the factors used in a factor-based VCV model are redundant and none of the asset returns are completely determined by the common factors, there will not be any portfolios that erroneously appear to be riskless. Therefore, a factor-based VCV matrix approach may result in some portfolios that erroneously appear to be riskless if any asset returns can be completely determined by the common factors or some of the factors are redundant.

A is incorrect because shrinkage estimation of VCV matrices will increase the efficiency of the estimates versus the sample VCV matrix, because its mean squared error (MSE) will in general be smaller than the MSE of the (unbiased) sample VCV matrix. Efficiency in this context means a smaller MSE.

B is incorrect because, although the proposed approach is not reliable, the reason is not that the sample VCV matrix is biased and inconsistent; on the contrary, it is unbiased and consistent. Rather, the estimate of the VCV matrix is not reliable because the number of observations is not at least 10 times the number of assets (i.e., with 10 years of monthly return data, there are only 120 observations, but the rule of thumb suggests there should be at least 200 observations for 20 asset classes).

20. B is correct. Bader expects the equity market in Country C (an emerging market) to become more fully integrated with the global market while Country A (a developed market) remains highly integrated. All else being equal, the Singer–Terhaar model implies that when a market becomes more globally integrated (segmented), its required return should decline (rise). As prices adjust to a lower (higher) required return, the market should deliver an even higher (lower) return than was previously expected or required by the market. Therefore, the allocation to markets that are moving toward integration should be increased. If a market is moving toward integration, its increased allocation will come at the expense of markets that are already highly integrated. This will typically entail a shift from developed markets to emerging markets.

21. B is correct. Country A's long-term corporate earnings growth rate of 4% per year is equal to the expected nominal GDP growth rate of 4%, which is an economically plausible long-run assumption. The only very long-run assumptions that are consistent with economically plausible relationships are %ΔE = Nominal GDP growth, %ΔS = 0, and %ΔP/E = 0, where %ΔE is the expected nominal earnings growth rate, %ΔS is the expected percentage change in shares outstanding, and %ΔP/E is the expected percentage change in the price-to-earnings ratio.

A is incorrect because a 2% rate of net share repurchases would eventually eliminate all shares, which is not an economically plausible very long-run assumption. The only very long-run assumptions that are consistent with economically plausible relationships are %ΔE = Nominal GDP growth, %ΔS = 0, and %ΔP/E = 0, where %ΔE is the expected nominal earnings growth rate, %ΔS is the expected percentage change in shares outstanding, and %ΔP/E is the expected percentage change in the price-to-earnings ratio.

C is incorrect because Country A's perpetually rising P/E would lead to an arbitrarily high price per currency unit of earnings per share. The only very long-run assumptions that are consistent with economically plausible relationships are %ΔE = Nominal GDP growth, %ΔS = 0, %ΔP/E = 0, where %ΔE is the expected nominal earnings growth rate, %ΔS is the expected percentage change in shares outstanding, and %ΔP/E is the expected percentage change in the price-to-earnings ratio.

22. A is correct. Per capita income for Country B has been falling, which is a potential source of political stress.

B is incorrect because the persistent current account deficit has been below 2% of GDP. Persistent current account deficits greater than 4% of GDP probably indicate a lack of competitiveness.

C is incorrect because Country B has been transitioning to International Financial Reporting Standards, with full convergence expected within two years, which is a positive development for better accounting standards.

23. A is correct. Bader should reallocate capital from Country A, which is expected to have a secularly rising current account deficit, to Country C, which is expected to have a secularly rising current account surplus. A rising current account deficit will tend to put upward pressure on real required returns and downward pressure on asset prices, whereas a rising current account surplus (or narrowing deficit) will put downward pressure on real required returns and upward pressure on asset prices. Analysts should consider reallocation of portfolio assets from countries with secularly rising current account deficits to those with secularly rising current account surpluses (or narrowing deficits).

24. A is correct. Purchasing power parity implies that the value of Country A's currency will decline. Inflation for Country A is expected to rise relative to global inflation. Purchasing power parity implies that the expected percentage change in Country A's exchange rate

should be equal to the difference in expected inflation rates. If Country A's inflation is rising relative to global inflation, then the currency will be expected to depreciate.

B is incorrect because purchasing power parity implies that the value of Country B's currency will remain stable. Inflation for Country B is expected to keep pace with global inflation. Purchasing power parity implies that the expected percentage change in Country B's exchange rate should be equal to the difference in expected inflation rates. If Country B's inflation is keeping pace with global inflation, then the exchange rate will be expected to stay the same, corresponding to a stable value of Country B's currency.

C is incorrect because purchasing power parity implies that the value of Country C's currency will rise. Inflation for Country C is expected to fall relative to global inflation. Purchasing power parity implies that the expected percentage change in Country C's exchange rate should be equal to the difference in expected inflation rates. If Country C's inflation is falling relative to global inflation, then the currency will be expected to appreciate.

25. B is correct. Hot money is flowing out of Country B; thus, Country B's central bank is the most likely to sell foreign currency (thereby draining domestic liquidity) to limit/avoid depreciation of the domestic currency and buy government securities (thereby providing liquidity) to sterilize the impact on bank reserves and interest rates.

   A is incorrect because Country A is not experiencing hot money flows and, therefore, would not need to sterilize the impact of money flows on domestic liquidity.

   C is incorrect because hot money is flowing into Country C; thus, Country C's central bank is most likely to sell government securities to limit the growth of bank reserves and/or maintain a target level of interest rates.

26. C is correct. Public debt makes up the majority of Country C's currency portfolio, which is the least supportive flow (or holding) to a currency. Public debt is less supportive because it has to be serviced and must be either repaid or refinanced, potentially triggering a crisis. Some types of flows and holdings are considered to be more or less supportive of the currency. Investments in private equity represent long-term capital committed to the market and are most supportive of the currency. Public equity would likely be considered the next most supportive of the currency. Debt investments are the least supportive of the currency.

ASSET ALLOCATION TO ALTERNATIVE INVESTMENTS

LEARNING OUTCOMES

The candidate should be able to:

- explain the roles that alternative investments play in multi-asset portfolios;
- compare alternative investments and bonds as risk mitigators in relation to a long equity position;
- compare traditional and risk-based approaches to defining the investment opportunity set, including alternative investments;
- discuss investment considerations that are important in allocating to different types of alternative investments;
- discuss suitability considerations in allocating to alternative investments;
- discuss approaches to asset allocation to alternative investments;
- discuss the importance of liquidity planning in allocating to alternative investments;
- discuss considerations in monitoring alternative investment programs.

SUMMARY OVERVIEW

- Allocations to alternatives are believed to increase a portfolio's risk-adjusted return. An investment in alternatives typically fulfills one or more of four roles in an investor's portfolio: capital growth, income generation, risk diversification, and/or safety.
- Private equity investments are generally viewed as return enhancers in a portfolio of traditional assets.

- Long/short equity strategies are generally believed to deliver equity-like returns with less than full exposure to the equity premium. Short-biased equity strategies are expected to lower a portfolio's overall equity beta while producing some measure of alpha. Arbitrage and event-driven strategies are expected to provide equity-like returns with little to no correlation with traditional asset classes.
- Real assets (e.g., commodities, farmland, timber, energy, and infrastructure assets) are generally perceived to provide a hedge against inflation.
- Timber investments provide both growth and inflation-hedging properties.
- Commodities (e.g., metals, energy, livestock, and agricultural commodities) serve as a hedge against inflation and provide a differentiated source of alpha. Certain commodity investments serve as safe havens in times of crisis.
- Farmland investing may have a commodity-like profile or a commercial real-estate-like profile.
- Energy investments are generally considered a real asset as the investor owns the mineral rights to commodities that are correlated with inflation factors.
- Infrastructure investments tend to generate stable/modestly growing income and to have high correlation with overall inflation.
- Real estate strategies range from core to opportunistic and are believed to provide protection against unanticipated increases in inflation. Core real estate strategies are more income-oriented, while opportunistic strategies rely more heavily on capital appreciation.
- Bonds have been a more effective volatility mitigator than alternatives over shorter time horizons.
- The traditional approaches to defining asset classes are easy to communicate and implement. However, they tend to over-estimate portfolio diversification and obscure primary drivers of risk.
- Typical risk factors applied to alternative investments include equity, size, value, liquidity, duration, inflation, credit spread, and currency. A benefit of the risk factor approach is that every asset class can be described using the same framework.
- Risk factor–based approaches have certain limitations. A framework with too many factors is difficult to administer and interpret, but too small a set of risk factors may not accurately describe the characteristics of alternative asset classes. Risk factor sensitivities are highly sensitive to the historical look-back period.
- Investors with less than a 15-year investment horizon should generally avoid investments in private real estate, private real asset, and private equity funds.
- Investors must consider whether they have the necessary skills, expertise, and resources to build an alternative investment program internally. Investors without a strong governance program are less likely to develop a successful alternative investment program.
- Reporting for alternative funds is often less transparent than investors are accustomed to seeing on their stock and bond portfolios. For many illiquid strategies, reporting is often received well past typical monthly or quarter-end deadlines. Full, position-level transparency is rare in many alternative strategies.
- Three primary approaches are used to determine the desired allocation to the alternative asset classes:
  - Monte Carlo simulation may be used to generate return scenarios that relax the assumption of normally distributed returns.
  - Optimization techniques, which incorporate downside risk or take into account skew, may be used to enhance the asset allocation process.
  - Risk factor–based approaches to alternative asset allocation can be applied to develop more robust asset allocation proposals.

- Two key analytical challenges in modelling allocations to alternatives include stale and/or artificially smoothed returns and return distributions that exhibit significant skewness and fat tails (or excess kurtosis).
- Artificially smoothed returns can be detected by testing the return stream for serial correlation. The analyst needs to unsmooth the returns to get a more accurate representation of the risk and return characteristics of the asset class.
- Skewness and kurtosis can be dealt with by using empirically observed asset returns because they incorporate the actual distribution. Advanced mathematical or statistical models can also be used to capture the true behavior of alternative asset classes.
- Applications of Monte Carlo simulation in allocating to alternative investments include:
  1) simulating skewed and fat-tailed financial variables by estimating the behavior of factors and/or assets in low-volatility regimes and high-volatility regimes, then generating scenarios using the different means and covariances estimated under the different regimes; and
  2) simulating portfolio outcomes (+/− 1 standard deviation) to estimate the likelihood of falling short of the investment objectives.
- Unconstrained mean–variance optimization (MVO) often leads to portfolios dominated by cash and fixed income at the low-risk end of the spectrum and by private equity at the high-risk end of the spectrum. Some investors impose minimum and maximum constraints on asset classes. Slight changes in the input variables could lead to substantial changes in the asset allocations.
- Mean–CVaR optimization may be used to identify allocations that minimize downside risk rather than simply volatility.
- Investors may choose to optimize allocations to risk factors rather than asset classes. These allocations, however, must be implemented using asset classes. Portfolios with similar risk factor exposures can have vastly different asset allocations.
- Some caveats with respect to risk factor–based allocations are that investors may hold different definitions for a given risk factor, correlations among risk factors may shift under changing market conditions, and some factor sensitivities are very unstable.
- Cash flow and commitment-pacing models enable investors in private alternatives to better manage their portfolio liquidity and set realistic annual commitment targets to reach the desired asset allocation.
- An alternative investment program should be monitored relative to the goals established for the alternative investment program, not simply relative to a benchmark. The investor must monitor developments in the relevant markets to ensure that the fundamental thesis underlying the decision to invest remains intact.
- Two common benchmarking approaches to benchmarking alternative investments—custom index proxies and peer group comparisons—have significant limitations.
- IRRs are sensitive to the timing of cash flows into and out of the fund. Two managers may have similar portfolios but different return profiles depending on their capital call and distribution schedule.
- Pricing issues can distort reported returns and the associated risk metrics, such as betas, correlations, and Sharpe ratios.
- Monitoring of the firm and the investment process are particularly important in alternative investment structures where the manager cannot be terminated easily. Key elements to monitor include key person risk, alignment of interests, style drift, risk management, client/asset turnover, client profile, and service providers.

PROBLEMS

The following information relates to Questions 1–8.

Kevin Kroll is the chair of the investment committee responsible for the governance of the Shire Manufacturing Corporation (SMC) defined benefit pension plan. The pension fund is currently fully funded and has followed an asset mix of 60% public equities and 40% bonds since Kroll has been chair. Kroll meets with Mary Park, an actuarial and pension consultant, to discuss issues raised at the last committee meeting.

Kroll notes that the investment committee would like to explore the benefits of adding alternative investments to the pension plan's strategic asset allocation. Kroll states:

Statement 1: The committee would like to know which alternative asset would best mitigate the risks to the portfolio due to unexpected inflation and also have a relatively low correlation with public equities to provide diversification benefits.

The SMC pension plan has been able to fund the annual pension payments without any corporate contributions for a number of years. The committee is interested in potential changes to the asset mix that could increase the probability of achieving the long-term investment target return of 5.5% while maintaining the funded status of the plan. Park notes that fixed-income yields are expected to remain low for the foreseeable future. Kroll asks:

Statement 2: If the public equity allocation remains at 60%, is there a single asset class that could be used for the balance of the portfolio to achieve the greatest probability of maintaining the pension funding status over a long time horizon? Under this hypothetical scenario, the balance of the portfolio can be allocated to either bonds, hedge funds, or private equities.

Park confirms with Kroll that the committee has historically used a traditional approach to define the opportunity set based on distinct macroeconomic regimes, and she proposes that a risk-based approach might be a better method. Although the traditional approach is relatively powerful for its ability to handle liquidity and manager selection issues compared to a risk-based approach, they both acknowledge that a number of limitations are associated with the existing approach.

Park presents a report (Exhibit 1) that proposes a new strategic asset allocation for the pension plan. Kroll states that one of the concerns that the investment committee will have regarding the new allocation is that the pension fund needs to be able to fund an upcoming early retirement incentive program (ERIP) that SMC will be offering to its employees within the next two years. Employees who have reached the age of 55 and whose age added to the number of years of company service sum to 75 or more can retire 10 years early and receive the defined benefit pension normally payable at age 65.

EXHIBIT 1   Proposed Asset Allocation of SMC Defined Benefit Pension Plan

Asset Class	Public Equities	Broad Fixed Income	Private Equities	Hedge Funds	Public Real Estate	Total
Target	45%	25%	10%	10%	10%	100%
Range	35%–55%	15%–35%	0%–12%	0%–12%	0%–12%	–

Kroll and Park then discuss suitability considerations related to the allocation in Exhibit 1. Kroll understands that one of the drawbacks of including the proposed alternative asset classes is that daily reporting will no longer be available. Investment reports for alternatives will likely be received after monthly or quarter-end deadlines used for the plan's traditional investments. Park emphasizes that in a typical private equity structure, the pension fund makes a commitment of capital to a blind pool as part of the private investment partnership.

In order to explain the new strategic asset allocation to the investment committee, Kroll asks Park why a risk factor–based approach should be used rather than a mean–variance-optimization technique. Park makes the following statements:

Statement 3:   Risk factor–based approaches to asset allocation produce more robust asset allocation proposals.

Statement 4:   A mean–variance optimization typically overallocates to the private alternative asset classes due to stale pricing.

Park notes that the current macroeconomic environment could lead to a bear market within a few years. Kroll asks Park to discuss the potential impact on liquidity planning associated with the actions of the fund's general partners in the forecasted environment.

Kroll concludes the meeting by reviewing the information in Exhibit 2 pertaining to three potential private equity funds analyzed by Park. Park discloses the following due diligence findings from a recent manager search. Fund A retains administrators, custodians, and auditors with impeccable reputations; Fund B has achieved its performance in a manner that appears to conflict with its reported investment philosophy; and Fund C has recently experienced the loss of three key persons.

EXHIBIT 2   Potential Private Equity Funds, Internal Rate of Return (IRR)

Private Equity Fund	Fund A	Fund B	Fund C
5-year IRR	12.9%	13.2%	13.1%

1. Based on Statement 1, Park should recommend:
   A. hedge funds.
   B. private equities.
   C. commodity futures.
2. In answering the question raised in Statement 2, Park would *most likely* recommend:
   A. bonds.
   B. hedge funds.
   C. private equities.

3. A limitation of the existing approach used by the committee to define the opportunity set is that it:
   A. is difficult to communicate.
   B. overestimates the portfolio diversification.
   C. is sensitive to the historical look-back period.

4. Based on Exhibit 1 and the proposed asset allocation, the greatest risk associated with the ERIP is:
   A. liability.
   B. leverage.
   C. liquidity.

5. The suitability concern discussed by Kroll and Park *most likely* deals with:
   A. governance.
   B. transparency.
   C. investment horizon.

6. Which of Park's statements regarding the asset allocation approaches is correct?
   A. Only Statement 3
   B. Only Statement 4
   C. Both Statement 3 and Statement 4

7. Based on the forecasted environment, liquidity planning should take into account that general partners may:
   A. call capital at a slower pace.
   B. make distributions at a faster pace.
   C. exercise an option to extend the life of the fund.

8. Based on Exhibit 2 and Park's due diligence, the pension committee should consider investing in:
   A. Fund A.
   B. Fund B.
   C. Fund C.

The following information relates to Questions 9–13.

Eileen Gension is a portfolio manager for Zen-Alt Investment Consultants (Zen-Alt), which assists institutional investors with investing in alternative investments. Charles Smittand is an analyst at Zen-Alt and reports to Gension. Gension and Smittand discuss a new client, the Benziger University Endowment Fund (the fund), as well as a prospective client, the Opeptaja Pension Plan (the plan).

The fund's current portfolio is invested primarily in public equities, with the remainder invested in fixed income. The fund's investment objective is to support a 6% annual spending rate and to preserve the purchasing power of the asset base over a 10-year time horizon. The fund also wants to invest in assets that provide the highest amount of diversification against its dominant equity risk. Gension considers potential alternative investment options that would best meet the fund's diversification strategy.

In preparation for the first meeting between Zen-Alt and the fund, Gension and Smittand discuss implementing a short-biased equity strategy within the fund. Smittand makes the following three statements regarding short-biased equity strategies:

Statement 1:   Short-biased equity strategies generally provide alpha when used to diversify public equities.

Statement 2:   Short-biased equity strategies are expected to provide a higher reduction in volatility than bonds over a long time horizon.

Statement 3:   Short-biased equity strategies are expected to mitigate the risk of public equities by reducing the overall portfolio beta of the fund.

Gension directs Smittand to prepare asset allocation and portfolio characteristics data on three alternative portfolios. The fund's risk profile is one factor that potential lenders consider when assigning a risk rating to the university. A loan covenant with the university's primary lender states that a re-evaluation of the university's creditworthiness is triggered if the fund incurs a loss greater than 20% over any one-year period. Smittand states that the recommended asset allocation should achieve the following three goals, in order of priority and importance:

- Minimize the probability of triggering the primary lender's loan covenant.
- Minimize the probability of purchasing power impairment over a 10-year horizon.
- Maximize the probability of achieving a real return target of 6% over a 10-year horizon.

Smittand provides data for three alternative portfolios, which are presented in Exhibits 3 and 4.

EXHIBIT 3   Asset Allocation

Alternative Portfolio	Cash	Public Equity	Gov't.	Credit	Hedge Fund	Real Estate	Private Equity
A	4.0%	35.0%	6.0%	5.0%	20.0%	10.0%	20.0%
B	2.0%	40.0%	8.0%	3.0%	15.0%	7.0%	25.0%
C	1.0%	50.0%	3.0%	6.0%	10.0%	0.0%	30.0%

EXHIBIT 4   Portfolio Characteristics

Alternative Portfolio	1-Year 99% VaR	1-Year 99% CVaR	Probability of Meeting 6% Real Return (10-Year Horizon)	Probability of Purchasing Power Impairment (10-Year Horizon)
A	−16.3%	−19.4%	56.1%	2.5%
B	−17.4%	−20.6%	58.8%	2.8%
C	−19.3%	−22.7%	61.0%	4.0%

Notes:
- One-year horizon 99% VaR: the lowest return over any one-year period at a 99% confidence level
- One-year horizon 99% CVaR: the expected return if the return falls below the 99% VaR threshold
- Probability of purchasing power impairment: the probability of losing 40% of the fund's purchasing power over 10 years, after consideration of new gifts received by the fund, spending from the fund, and total returns

Gension next meets with the investment committee (IC) of the Opeptaja Pension Plan to discuss new opportunities in alternative investments. The plan is a $1 billion public pension fund that is required to provide detailed reports to the public and operates under specific government guidelines. The plan's IC adopted a formal investment policy that specifies an investment horizon of 20 years. The plan has a team of in-house analysts with significant experience in alternative investments.

During the meeting, the IC indicates that it is interested in investing in private real estate. Gension recommends a real estate investment managed by an experienced team with a proven track record. The investment will require multiple capital calls over the next few years. The IC proceeds to commit to the new real estate investment and seeks advice on liquidity planning related to the future capital calls.

9. Which asset class would *best* satisfy the Fund's diversification strategy?
   A. Private equity
   B. Private real estate
   C. Absolute return hedge fund
10. Which of Smittand's statements regarding short-biased equity strategies is *incorrect?*
    A. Statement 1
    B. Statement 2
    C. Statement 3
11. Based on Exhibit 4, which alternative portfolio should Gension recommend for the fund given Smittand's stated three goals?
    A. Portfolio A
    B. Portfolio B
    C. Portfolio C
12. Which of the following investor characteristics would *most likely* be a primary concern for the plan's IC with respect to investing in alternatives?
    A. Governance
    B. Transparency
    C. Investment horizon
13. With respect to liquidity planning relating to the plan's new real estate investment, Gension should recommend that the fund set aside appropriate funds and invest them in:
    A. 100% REITs.
    B. 100% cash equivalents.
    C. 80% cash equivalents and 20% REITs.

The following information relates to Questions 14–15.

Ingerðria Greslö is an adviser with an investment management company and focuses on asset allocation for the company's high-net-worth investors. She prepares for a meeting with Maarten Pua, a new client who recently inherited a $10 million portfolio solely comprising public equities.

Greslö meets with Pua and proposes that she create a multi-asset portfolio by selling a portion of his equity holdings and investing the proceeds in another asset class. Greslö advises Pua that his investment objective should be to select an asset class that has a high potential to fulfill two functional roles: risk diversification and capital growth. Greslö suggests the following three asset classes:

- Public real estate
- Private real assets (timber)
- Equity long/short hedge funds

14. **Determine** which asset class is *most likely* to meet Pua's investment objective. **Justify** your response.

Determine which asset class is *most likely* to meet Pua's investment objective. (Circle one.)	**Justify** your response.
Public Real Estate	
Private Real Assets (Timber)	
Equity Long/Short Hedge Funds	

Five years after his first meeting with Pua, Greslö monitors a private real estate investment that Pua has held for one year. Until recently, the investment had been managed by a local real estate specialist who had a competitive advantage in this market; the specialist's strategy was to purchase distressed local residential housing properties, make strategic property improvements, and then sell them. Pua is one of several clients who have invested in this opportunity.

Greslö learns that the specialist recently retired and the investment is now managed by a national real estate company. The company has told investors that it now plans to invest throughout the region in both distressed housing and commercial properties. The company also lengthened the holding period for each investment property from the date of the initial capital call because of the complexity of the property renovations, and it altered the interim profit distribution targets.

15. **Discuss** the qualitative risk issues that have *most likely* materialized over the past year.

The following information relates to Questions 16–18.

The Ælfheah Group is a US-based company with a relatively small pension plan. Ælfheah's investment committee (IC), whose members collectively have a relatively basic understanding of the investment process, has agreed that Ælfheah is willing to accept modest returns while the IC gains a better understanding of the process Two key investment considerations for the IC are maintaining low overhead costs and minimizing taxes in the portfolio. Ælfheah has not been willing to incur the costs of in-house investment resources.

Qauhtèmoc Ng is the investment adviser for Ælfheah. He discusses with the IC its goal of diversifying Ælfheah's portfolio to include alternative assets. Ng suggests considering the following potential investment vehicles:

- Publicly traded US REIT
- Relative value hedge fund
- Tax-efficient angel investment

Ng explains that for the relative value hedge fund alternative, Ælfheah would be investing alongside tax-exempt investors.

16. **Determine** which of the potential investment vehicles *best* meets the investment considerations for Ælfheah. **Justify** your response. **Explain** for *each* investment not selected why the investment considerations are not met.

Determine which of the potential investment vehicles *best* meets the investment considerations for Ælfheah. (Circle one.)	**Justify** your response.	**Explain** for *each* investment not selected why the investment considerations are not met.
Publicly traded US REIT		
Relative value hedge fund		
Tax-efficient angel investment		

Ng and the IC review the optimal approach to determine the asset allocation for Ælfheah, including the traditional and risk-based approaches to defining the investment opportunity set.

17. **Determine** which approach to determine the asset allocation is *most appropriate* for Ælfheah. **Justify** your response.

Determine which approach to determine the asset allocation is *most appropriate* for Ælfheah. (Circle one.)	**Justify** your response.
Traditional	
Risk based	

The following year, Ng and the IC review the portfolio's performance. The IC has gained a better understanding of the investment process. The portfolio is meeting Ælfheah's liquidity needs, and Ng suggests that Ælfheah would benefit from diversifying into an additional alternative asset class. After discussing suitable investment vehicles for the proposed alternative asset class, Ng proposes the following three investment vehicles for further review:

- Funds of funds (FOFs)
- Separately managed accounts (SMAs)
- Undertakings for collective investment in transferable securities (UCITS)

18. **Determine** the investment vehicle that would be *most appropriate* for Ælfheah's proposed alternative asset class. **Justify** your response.

Determine the investment vehicle that would be *most appropriate* for Ælfheah's proposed alternative asset class. (Circle one.)	**Justify** your response.
FOFs	
SMAs	
UCITS	

The following information relates to Questions 19–20.

Mbalenhle Calixto is a global institutional portfolio manager who prepares for an annual meeting with the investment committee (IC) of the Estevão University Endowment. The endowment has €450 million in assets, and the current asset allocation is 42% equities, 22% fixed income, 19% private equity, and 17% hedge funds.

The IC's primary investment objective is to maximize returns subject to a given level of volatility. A secondary objective is to avoid a permanent loss of capital, and the IC has indicated to Calixto its concern about left-tail risk. Calixto considers two asset allocation approaches for the endowment: mean–variance optimization (MVO) and mean–CVaR (conditional value at risk) optimization.

19. **Determine** the asset allocation approach that is *most suitable* for the Endowment. **Justify** your response.

Determine the asset allocation approach that is *most suitable* for the Endowment. (Circle one.)	**Justify** your response.
MVO	
Mean–CVaR optimization	

Calixto reviews the endowment's future liquidity requirements and analyzes one of its holdings in a private distressed debt fund. He notes the following about the fund:

- As of the most recent year end:
  - The NAV of the endowment's investment in the fund was €25,000,000.
  - All capital had been called.
- At the end of the current year, Calixto expects a distribution of 18% to be paid.
- Calixto estimates an expected growth rate of 11% for the fund.

20. **Calculate** the expected NAV of the fund at the end of the current year.

CHAPTER **8**

ASSET ALLOCATION TO ALTERNATIVE INVESTMENTS

SOLUTIONS

1. C is correct. Real assets (which include energy, infrastructure, timber, commodities, and farmland) are generally believed to mitigate the risks to the portfolio arising from unexpected inflation. Commodities act as a hedge against a core constituent of inflation measures. Rather than investing directly in the actual commodities, commodity futures may be incorporated using a managed futures strategy. In addition, the committee is looking for an asset class that has a low correlation with public equities, which will provide diversification benefits. Commodities are regarded as having much lower correlation coefficients with public equities than with private equities and hedge funds. Therefore, commodities will provide the greatest potential to fulfill the indicated role and to diversify public equities.

2. C is correct. When projecting expected returns, the order of returns from highest to lowest is typically regarded as private equities, hedge funds, bonds. Therefore, the probability of achieving the highest portfolio return while maintaining the funded status of the plan would require the use of private equities in conjunction with public equities. In addition, private equities have a high/strong potential to fulfill the role of capital growth. Fixed-income investments are expected to have a high/strong potential to fulfill the role of safety.

3. B is correct. A traditional approach has been used to define the opportunity set based on different macroeconomic conditions. The primary limitations of traditional approaches are that they overestimate the portfolio diversification and obscure the primary drivers of risk.

4. C is correct. With the introduction of the early retirement incentive plan (ERIP), the defined benefit pension plan will likely be called upon to make pension payments earlier than originally scheduled. As a result, the near term liquidity of the plan is the greatest risk arising from the addition of the alternative asset classes (e.g., private equities, hedge funds, and real estate). Investments in alternatives, such as private equities, can take upwards of five years to reach a full commitment and potentially another decade to unwind.

5. B is correct. The pension plan's investment in private equities via a blind pool presents the prospect that less than perfect transparency will be associated with the underlying holdings of the alternative asset manager. Capital is committed for an investment in a portfolio

of assets that are not specified in advance. In addition, reporting for alternative funds is often less transparent than investors are accustomed to seeing on their stock and bond portfolios.

6. C is correct. Statement 3 is correct because risk factor-based approaches to asset allocation can be applied to develop more robust asset allocations. Statement 4 is correct because a mean–variance optimization typically overallocates to the private alternative asset classes, partly because of underestimated risk due to stale pricing and the assumption that returns are normally distributed

7. C is correct. Park notes that the current macroeconomic environment could lead to a bear market within a few years. Liquidity planning should take into account that under a scenario in which public equities and fixed-income investments are expected to perform poorly, general partners may exercise an option to extend the life of the fund.

8. A is correct. Fund A should be selected based on both quantitative and qualitative factors. Fund A has a five-year IRR (12.9%) that is slightly lower than, but comparable to, both Fund B (13.2%) and Fund C (13.1%). Given the sensitivity to the timing of cash flows into and out of a fund associated with the IRR calculation, however, the final decision should not be based merely on quantitative returns. It is also important to monitor the investment process and the investment management firm itself, particularly in alternative investment structures. Considering the qualitative factors identified by Park, Fund A is the only fund with a strong, positive factor. It benefits from service providers (administrators, custodians, and auditors) with impeccable reputations. Fund B seems to be experiencing style drift, which suggests that the returns are not consistent with the manager's advertised investment edge (hence, a negative factor). Fund C has experienced the departure of key persons, which puts future fund returns in jeopardy (hence, a negative factor).

9. C is correct. An absolute return hedge fund has a greater potential to diversify the fund's dominant public equity risk than either private equity or private real estate. Absolute return hedge funds exhibit an equity beta that is often less than that of private equity or private real estate. Also, absolute return hedge funds tend to exhibit a high potential to diversify public equities, whereas equity long/short hedge funds exhibit a moderate potential to fulfill this role.

    A is incorrect because although private equity provides moderate diversification against public equity, an absolute return hedge fund has a greater potential to do so. The primary advantage of private equity is capital growth.

    B is incorrect because private real estate provides only moderate diversification against public equity, whereas absolute return hedge funds have a greater potential to do so. The primary advantage of private real estate is income generation.

10. B is correct. While bonds reduce the probability of achieving a target return over time, they have been more effective as a volatility mitigator than alternatives over an extended period of time.

    A is incorrect because Statement 1 is correct. Short-biased strategies are expected to provide some measure of alpha in addition to lowering a portfolio's overall equity beta.

    C is incorrect because Statement 3 is correct. Short-biased equity strategies help reduce an equity-dominated portfolio's overall beta. Short-biased strategies are believed to deliver equity-like returns with less-than-full exposure to the equity premium but with an additional source of return that might come from the manager's shorting of individual stocks.

11. A is correct. Among the three portfolios, Portfolio A minimizes the probability of triggering the primary lender's loan covenant, which is the highest-priority goal, because it has the lowest one-year 99% CVaR, –19.4%. Portfolio A also has the lowest probability of purchasing power impairment over a 10-year horizon (2.5%). While Portfolio A has the lowest probability of achieving a real return target of 6% over a 10-year horizon (56.1%), that is the least important goal to be met. Therefore, Gension should recommend Portfolio A for the fund.

   B is incorrect because Portfolio B has a one-year 99% CVaR of –20.6%, which crosses the loan covenant threshold of a 20% loss. Portfolio A is the only one that satisfies the most important goal and is the portfolio least likely to trigger the loan covenant. Since Portfolio B does not achieve the most important goal of minimizing the probability of triggering the primary lender's loan covenant, Portfolio B should not be the recommended portfolio.

   C is incorrect because despite the fact that Portfolio C has the highest probability of meeting the 6% real return over a 10-year horizon, 61.0%, it also has a one-year 99% CVaR of –22.7% and thus the highest probability of triggering the loan covenant. Portfolio A is the only one that satisfies the most important goal and is the portfolio least likely to trigger the loan covenant. Since Portfolio C does not achieve the most important goal of minimizing the probability of triggering the primary lender's loan covenant, Portfolio C should not be the recommended portfolio.

12. B is correct. As a public pension fund that is required to provide detailed reports to the public, a primary concern for the IC is transparency. Investors in alternative investments must be comfortable with less than 100% transparency in their holdings. Private equity funds often necessitate buying into a "blind pool." Although an investor can look at the assets acquired in a manager's previous funds, there is no assurance that future investments will exactly replicate the previous funds.

   A is incorrect because the IC has a formal investment policy, as well as an in-house team with experience in alternatives and the knowledge and capacity to critically evaluate alternative investments.

   C is incorrect because the IC has a long-term investment horizon. While investors with less than a 15-year horizon should generally avoid investing in alternatives, the IC has a 20-year investment horizon that should easily accommodate an investment in private equity.

13. A is correct. REITs are most appropriate for funds committed to private real estate investments since they will have the most similar return and risk characteristics and will help maintain the strategic asset allocation of the plan. Although cash equivalents have less volatility over a short-term horizon, they are less likely to meet the plan's long-term return objectives.

   B is incorrect because the opportunity cost of being out of the markets over the next few years during the capital call period makes cash equivalents an inappropriate investment. Although cash equivalents have lower volatility, which is often desirable over a short-term period, they will not help the plan meet its long-term return objectives.

   C is incorrect because, although REITs will have the return and risk characteristics most similar to private real estate, a 20% allocation is not large enough to achieve the plan's long-term return objectives. The 80% allocation to cash equivalents will greatly affect the return, making the plan less likely to meet the long-term return objectives.

14.

Determine which asset class is *most likely* to meet Pua's investment objective. (Circle one.)	**Justify** your response.
Public Real Estate	• Timber exhibits a low correlation with public equities and can fulfill the functional role of risk diversification. • Timber provides high long-term returns and can fulfill the functional role of capital growth. Private real assets (timber) is the asset class most likely to meet Pua's objective. Private real assets, such as timber, tend to exhibit a low correlation with public equities and therefore have a high potential to fulfill the functional role of risk diversification in Pua's current all-equity portfolio. In addition, timber has a high potential to fulfill the functional role of capital growth in the portfolio since growth is provided by the underlying biological growth of the tree as well as through appreciation in the underlying land value.
Private Real Assets (Timber)	
Equity Long/Short Hedge Funds	Compared with timber, public real estate as an asset class would likely offer less opportunity for capital growth and lower diversification benefits. Also, equity long/short hedge funds as an asset class would provide a moderate degree of risk diversification in Pua's all-equity portfolio but do not carry significant capital growth potential.

15.

- Pua's investment has been affected by key person risk as shown by the effect of the management change.
- Style drift has occurred as shown by the change from a local to a regional investment strategy and the expansion of the investment strategy to include commercial properties.
- The risk of the investment has changed owing to the added complexity of the property renovations.
- The longer holding periods and the change in interim profit distribution targets will affect this investment.
- Client/asset turnover following the management change may now affect the performance of the investment.
- The management change may alter the client profile, which could have a negative effect on investment performance.

Qualitative considerations can lead to a better understanding of the revised strategy for the investment and whether this investment remains suitable for Pua. Pua's investment has been affected by key person risk as shown by the management change from the local manager to a national company. Style drift has occurred as shown by the change from a local to a regional investment strategy and the expansion of the strategy to include commercial properties.

The risk of the investment has changed because of the added complexity of the renovations, and monitoring the company's risk management will be important for Greslö as she manages Pua's portfolio. Monitoring of the private real estate investment has revealed discrepancies in the new management strategy of the national company relative to the initial investment strategy of the local manager, including the longer holding periods and the changed interim profit distribution targets. Client/asset turnover following the management change may now significantly affect the performance of the investment. Finally, the change in management may alter the client profile, which could have a negative effect on investment performance.

16.

Determine which of the potential investment vehicles *best* meets the investment considerations for Ælfheah. (Circle one.)	**Justify** your response.	**Explain** for *each* investment not selected why the investment considerations are not met.
Publicly traded US REIT	The publicly traded US REIT offers tax advantages to Ælfheah from the depreciation of its US real estate assets. The depreciation would help offset income received on those assets. In addition, the REIT would not require an in-house management team; thus, Ælfheah can maintain low overhead costs.	
Relative value hedge fund		The relative value hedge fund is unlikely to be a tax-efficient strategy for Ælfheah. This tax inefficiency is seen frequently with many hedge fund strategies, especially those funds and fund companies where tax-exempt investors dominate the client base. The fund manager may be insensitive to tax considerations for a taxable investor such as Ælfheah.

Tax-efficient angel investment		The tax-efficient angel investment is a specialized investment that will require a highly customized investment approach. Researching and managing this type of investment will require an in-house team to locate and supervise these more specialized investments. Adding these resources would increase overhead costs and violate the IC's investment consideration of maintaining low overhead costs.

17.

Determine which approach to determine the asset allocation is *most appropriate* for Ælfheah. (Circle one.)	**Justify** your response.
Traditional	• The traditional approach is more appropriate since describing the roles of various asset classes is intuitive. • This approach will be easier for Ng to explain to the IC, whose members have only a basic understanding of the investment process. • This approach will make it easier to identify relevant mandates for the portfolio's alternative investments. • Since Ælfheah seeks to maintain low overhead costs, the risk-based approach would not be appropriate. The traditional approach is more appropriate for Ælfheah. The IC is less sophisticated in its understanding of alternative investments but may have some familiarity with the traditional asset class-based approach. Listing the roles of various asset classes will be more intuitive and easy for Ng to explain to the IC.
Risk based	The traditional approach has relevance for the IC's liquidity and operational considerations. This approach will make it easier to identify relevant mandates for the alternative investments in the portfolio. The traditional approach also will allow the IC to obtain a better understanding of how various asset classes behave so that Ng can tailor the asset allocation to address any concerns. The traditional approach will be easier to implement, and the IC does not want to add costly in-house resources, which would likely be necessary with the risk-based approach.

18.

Determine the investment vehicle that would be *most appropriate* for Ælfheah's proposed alternative asset class. (Circle one.)	**Justify** your response.
FOFs	• An FOF would allow Ælfheah to co-invest with other investors in alternative investment opportunities for which Ælfheah might otherwise be too small to participate. • An in-house team would not be necessary to review and maintain an FOF, which uses an outside manager. • Ælfheah is unlikely to meet the very high minimum investment of an SMA, which may also require enhanced in-house investment resources. • Ælfheah does not need the higher liquidity of UCITS, which have a less attractive risk/return profile for Ælfheah's relatively small-sized portfolio. An FOF is the most appropriate investment vehicle for Ælfheah. This vehicle allows Ælfheah to co-invest alongside other investors in order to participate in alternative investment opportunities for which it would otherwise be too small to participate. An expert in-house team would not be necessary to review and maintain the types of investments in an FOF since this investment vehicle uses an outside manager.
SMAs	SMAs are available for certain large portfolios, such as those of large family offices or foundations, but it is unlikely that Ælfheah would meet the very high minimum investment requirement. This type of investment poses greater operational challenges for the investor; thus, an SMA may require enhanced in-house investment resources. UCITS are less appropriate for Ælfheah since the pension plan is a medium-sized (not small-sized) investor and its liquidity needs are being met. Ælfheah should instead invest in a vehicle that offers lower liquidity with a more attractive risk/return profile. Also, UCITS have regulatory restrictions that can make them more difficult for a fund manager to implement the desired investment strategy.
UCITS	

19.

Determine the asset allocation approach that is *most suitable* for the Endowment. (Circle one.)	**Justify** your response.
MVO	• Mean–CVaR will better address the IC's concern about left-tail risk (the risk of a permanent capital loss). • If the portfolio contains asset classes and investment strategies with negative skewness and long tails, CVaR optimization could materially alter the asset allocation decision. Given the IC's investment objectives for the endowment, using a mean–CVaR optimization approach is more suitable for determining the asset allocation. The IC has 36% of its portfolio invested in alternative assets, 19% in private equity, and 17% in hedge funds. Thus, the IC has a more sophisticated understanding of risk and will appreciate the more nuanced view of risk offered by mean–CVaR optimization. The portfolio has exposure to alternative investments, and the IC is concerned about left-tail risk (the risk of a permanent loss of capital), as indicated to Calixto. Thus, the asset allocation decision will be enhanced by the more detailed understanding of left-tail risk offered by mean–CVaR optimization relative to MVO. MVO cannot easily accommodate the characteristics of most alternative investments. MVO characterizes an asset's risk using standard deviation. Standard deviation, a one-dimensional view of risk, is a poor representation of the risk characteristics of alternative investments for which asset returns may be not normally distributed. MVO typically over-allocates to alternative asset classes, partly because risk is underestimated because of stale or infrequent pricing and the underlying assumption that returns are normally distributed.
Mean–CVaR optimization	An investor particularly concerned with the downside risk of a proposed asset allocation may choose to minimize the portfolio's CVaR rather than its volatility relative to a return target. If the portfolio contains asset classes and investment strategies with negative skewness and long tails, CVaR optimization could materially alter the asset allocation decision.

20. The expected NAV of the fund at the end of the current year is €25,258,050, calculated as follows:

First, the expected distribution at the end of the current year is calculated as

Expected distribution = [Prior-year NAV × (1 + Growth rate)] × (Distribution rate).

Expected distribution = [(€25,000,000 × 1.11) × 18%] = €4,995,000.

Therefore, the expected NAV of the fund at the end of the current year is

Expected NAV = [Prior-year NAV × (1 + Growth rate) + Capital contributions − Distributions)] × (1 + Growth rate).

Expected NAV = [(€25,000,000 × 1.11) + 0 − €4,995,000] × 1.11 = €25,258,050.

INTEGRATED CASES IN RISK MANAGEMENT: INSTITUTIONAL

LEARNING OUTCOMES

The candidate should be able to:

- discuss financial risks associated with the portfolio strategy of an institutional investor;
- discuss environmental and social risks associated with the portfolio strategy of an institutional investor;
- analyze and evaluate the financial and non-financial risk exposures in the portfolio strategy of an institutional investor;
- discuss various methods to manage the risks that arise on long-term direct investments of an institutional investor;
- evaluate strengths and weaknesses of an enterprise risk management system and recommend improvements.